Elk Hunting 201

Big Bulls…Essentials for a Successful Hunt

Jay Houston

www.ElkCamp.com

America's #1 Online Resource for Elk Hunters
Jackson Creek Publishers
Colorado Springs, Colorado 80920

ELK HUNTING 201

BIG BULLS...Essentials for a Successful Hunt

Jay Houston

Copyright © 2005 by Jay Houston / Author

Our magnificent cover photo is courtesy of Jim Christensen of Digital Image Photography.

Our new elk image logo is courtesy of Rusty Phelps. Rusty's work in Bronze, Oil, Acrylic, Pen and Ink, and Hydrastone are renowned throughout the West. We are grateful for this original work that Rusty created for ElkCamp.com.

All rights reserved. No part of the publication may be reproduced, stored in a retrieval system, or transmitted in any form or by any means—electronic, mechanical, digital, photocopy, recording, or any other—except for brief quotations in printed reviews, without the prior written permission of the author and publisher.

Printed in the United States of America

ISBN 0-9759319-1-1

Jackson Creek Publishers
8697 Bellcove Circle
Colorado Springs, Colorado 80920

TABLE OF CONTENTS

"The credit belongs to the man in the arena whose face is marred by dust and sweat and blood, who strives valiantly...who knows the great enthusiasms, the great devotions, who spends himself in a worthy cause, who at the best knows in the end the triumph of high achievement, and who at the worst, if he fails, fails while daring greatly, so that his place shall never be with those cold and timid souls who have known neither victory nor defeat."

President Theodore Roosevelt

"Brothers, whatever is true, whatever is noble, whatever is right, whatever is pure, whatever is lovely, whatever is admirable—if anything is excellent or praiseworthy—think about such things. Whatever you have learned or received from me, or seen in me—put it into practice. And the God of peace will be with you."

The Apostle Paul
Philippians 4: 8-9 NIV

Acknowledgements

I would like to thank those who helped to make our first book, *Elk Hunting 101, A Pocketbook Guide to Elk Hunting*, a huge success. Some have said that we knocked this one over the fence. Well I don't know about that, but so far it has exceeded all of our expectations and to all of those who helped to make this book a success, we are eternally grateful. When one sets out to tell a story or in this case write a book, there is never any assurance of how the audience will receive it. In an industry where a high percentage of projects fail to succeed, we are truly blessed by the victory we have experienced.

We want to thank some of those who have made this possible. First and foremost, Rae Ann and I thank God Almighty for gifting us, bringing us together, and showing us the way. We thank the thousands of readers who took a chance on us and purchased the book. We also thank the readers at ElkCamp.com who sent in their ideas and questions that helped to formulate much of the content. We want to thank the great team at the Rocky Mountain Elk Foundation for their generous encouragement and support. We want to thank the folks at Cabela's Wildlife Heritage Catalog and Sportsman's Warehouse for believing in us. Also our sincere thanks go out to Gerry Caillouet and Tracy Breene at God's Great Outdoors radio broadcast and web e-zine, Cris Draper and KSL 1160 Utah Outdoors radio, and of course my true friend, and loyal elk huntin' buddy Roger Medley of BackCountryBowhunting.com and HighCountry Ministries.

We also want to offer a very special thanks to some great friends who came to the rescue when I was in a world of hurt (you will read about this later in this book). Were it not for their selfless acts of mercy, my wife would have been even more concerned for my welfare and Elk Hunting 201 would surely have been delayed. A heartfelt thanks to Mike Hogan of A-Cent Aviation in Colorado Springs and Gary Erickson, who piloted Gary's Piper Saratoga II to Grand Junction and scooped my broken body out of there just minutes before Vice President Dick Cheney arrived in Air Force Two and the airfield was closed to all arrivals and departures. Thanks also to the folks at West Star Aviation and the men and women of the United States Secret Service for their understanding and generosity in allowing me to wait for my flight home in an area that was officially closed to unauthorized civilians at the time.

Rocky Mountain Elk Foundation

Whether you are an elk hunter or an elk lover, I encourage you to give thoughtful consideration to becoming a member of the Rocky Mountain Elk Foundation. As a member I believe that no other single organization has done more for elk and elk country. If we want to preserve elk then we must get involved personally and take measures to preserve elk habitat. The mission of the Elk Foundation is to ensure the future of elk, other wildlife and their habitat. Folks if you're serious about elk, this is not a difficult decision. You can make a difference. Please don't make the mistake of putting this decision off thinking someone else will step up to the plate. For our children and our grandchildren, this responsibility is yours and mine. Please join me in this most worthy endeavor. It is a small investment but the return will benefit many generations to come. Just pick up the phone and call 800-CALL-ELK and join today.

Why We Chose A Brief "Get to The Point" Format

Twenty-first century hunters are in many ways no different than any other twenty-first century folks. As such, most of us are perpetually in a hurry, have little perceived extra time, and we want information presented to us in a brief, concise, and interesting format. In other words, "give me the short version and get to the point."

Over the years I have read dozens of books on elk and big game hunting. Most of those books are lying right here on my desk. A well-known outdoorsman and first-class author wrote every one of these, and yet each conveys its story in a slightly different form.

Our *Elk Hunting 101 - 201 - 301* format is designed to help you learn to become a more successful elk hunter. Our goal is to educate while providing you this information accurately but as "to the point" as practical. We could ramble on about the subjects that we discuss, but we have chosen not to because we value your time plus one other very important reason. Every elk that you read about in a book is already hanging over some other guy's fireplace or is frozen solid in the form of roasts, steaks, and burger. Our job is to help prepare you for your next great hunt and all the future opportunities that you may encounter in elk country.

I hope you enjoy the read. From time to time I offer a brief tale if it helps to clarify or reinforce a point. I most certainly appreciate your graciousness and patience with my attempts at humor as well as those times where I may go a bit overboard trying to make a point.

God bless, enjoy the journey and safe hunting,

Jay

Chapter One

Veteran Elk Hunters Can Learn Too

If ever I needed proof positive that every elk hunter needs to push himself beyond the fundamentals and become equipped with as much knowledge of the elk and the environment in which they live as he can get; and that he must accept total responsibility for his own success and welfare while in the field; my personal experience during our 2004 elk hunt brought those fundamentals home in the form of painfully acquired yet valuable lessons that I will not soon forget.

Colorado's second combined rifle season in mid-October can be a challenging time to hunt elk for even the most experienced of elk hunters. The rut is usually over, an army of bowhunters, smoke-pole shooters and riflemen has assaulted the backcountry and pressured the elk from every direction imaginable since the end of August, and the really heavy snows often associated with later hunting seasons have yet to arrive and drive the elk out of their hideouts in the high country. I have been hunting elk for many years and truth-be-told, the 2004 season was as tough a hunt as I have ever experienced.

Our base camp in NW Colorado, 2004

Our gaggle of six hunters, beset with years of anticipation arrived at base camp alongside our guides and the camp cook about mid-afternoon on Sunday aboard a drained pack-string of horses and mules, rather trail weary ourselves after almost four hours in the saddle. Though we were sore of seat, we quickly unloaded the gear from the horses and immediately decided to head for the black timber just beyond camp to begin our search for those elusive branch-antlered beasts.

Four of the first five days of hunting met us with cooler temperatures, accompanied by ground-hugging jet stream like winds often blowing rain, sleet, snow or a mixture of all three sideways for much of the time. I remember sitting on the edge of a meadow surrounded by naked aspens one afternoon, hunkered down as low as I could get and listening to the never-ending wail of the wind just over my head.

Meadow where the wind howled all day, NW Colorado, 2004

It was like having one jet fighter after another make a low pass. I had thought about trying my cow call, but alas I had serious doubts that the elk could have heard a ship's foghorn in all that racket. I think you get the picture…hunting was very tough. A 360-class bull could have walked up right behind me and I could not have heard him. Clearly the elk didn't care for the weather any more than we did, because in five days of very hard hunting, my hunting partner, guide and I only managed to eyeball a young spike bull and a couple of cows between us. When the weather turns sour, the elk dig in, far back in the black timber and usually just wait it out.

Day after day our hope had been that the storms, lined up one behind the other, would abate, and we would catch the elk as they exited their hidey-holes in search of food and water. Unfortunately, Mother Nature had other ideas. But hey, that's elk hunting. It's what we as elk hunters sign on for, right?

One Bad Porcupine! This one is not ours but I trust you will get the point.

Late in the afternoon on our fifth day of trying to pry elk out of the quakie patches and black timber of the Routt National Forest in Northwest Colorado, "Murphy" (of Murphy's Law) reared his head in the form of a single twenty-pound "horse-eating" porcupine who took it upon himself to single-handedly "assault"— the horse version of the story — three fifteen-hundred pound horses and as many fully armed hunters. Can you visualize this picture? Three huge men armed to the teeth, atop three massive horses strung out in a line going up the trail to the top of a ridge, when out strolls this little black prickly demon, more or less minding his own business. Actually, I never saw the thorny little devil, but his mere presence in close proximity to our guide's lead horse, as innocent as it may have been, began a shattering chain of events that has forever changed my life.

Photo of the three guilty critters before the rodeo, NW Colorado, 2004

Have you ever watched a movie where the filmmaker uses slow motion to let the viewer see certain details that might go unnoticed at normal speed? Folks, let me tell you, it really happens. While some of the details are still a bit fuzzy, I can still see the lead horse (in slow-motion) come to a decision that all was not well in her world, and that she would rather begin her exit of the county on two legs (the rear ones) rather than the conventional four. Keep in mind: I have still not seen prickly little "Mr. Murphy", only the rodeo that he has started. In the space of what I think was just a few seconds, all three horses, one after the other like a cascading set of dominoes had gone absolutely stark raving nuts, and departed the area for parts unknown, depositing all three of their riders on the ground in various states of disrepair. Angel, the lead horse had let her rider, our guide, almost dismount before deciding to make a beeline down the mountain while our guide was still trying to get his foot out of the stirrup, flipping him like a cheap burger in the process. Horse number two decided to begin his escape by charging through a grove of aspens, like Jeremiah Johnson racing back to the cabin. Most of the trees were barely far enough apart for the horse to get through, much less a horse with a large newbie rider hanging onto his back for dear life. Folks it looked just like it does on Pro Rodeo on TV. Not wanting to be left out of all the excitement, my mount Conway, who in all fairness had been a real gentleman for five days, decided that he didn't want any part of whatever was going on up the trail and decided like horse number one to initiate his immediate bail out on two legs rather than four as well.

Folks, if you have never seen the view from the back of a horse whose feet are in the air over your head while pirouetting on his back legs...count yourself blessed. As my steed completed his 180-degree turn, he threw his head violently to one side snatching the reins from my hands leaving me with absolutely no control over where he was going. When finally his front legs were reunited with Mother earth, all he and I could see were the other two horses going down the mountain like they were snake bit.

Not caring at all to try to hang onto a run-away horse going hell-bent for the lead in a three horse race down the mountain with no reins, I decided it was time for me to bail out while I still had a vote. At least I think it was my decision, but perhaps not. That part is also still a little fuzzy too. Either way I ended up hitting the ground like a sack of cheap bricks on my right side. I continued to lay still for about a minute making sure I was still alive. A brief examination confirmed my fears that most of my body parts were still working but a few...were not working at all. When the fog in my head began to clear I could see Joe Novosel, my hunting partner from Dutch Harbor, Alaska about a hundred yards down the mountain trying to stand up, then fall down for a while, and then finally stagger to something remotely resembling vertical again. Once Randy, our guide, was able to stand, he staggered up and asked me if I was ok? With all the clarity of a coastal morning fog bank, I told him that I was alive at least, but that my right arm wasn't working at all. Assuming that I would be ok for a few minutes, he walked down the hill to see what kind of shape Joe was in. I guess he was satisfied that we were both ok for the time being, so he set off looking for the horses. For what seemed like the next few hours that was the last either Joe or I saw of another human being.

Like so many other hunters, I grew up reading *Outdoor Life Magazine*. As a youngster growing up in the South, I was fascinated by tales of massive grizzlies roaming the wilds of Wyoming and the majestic elk and mule deer that lived high in the Rockies. Having been no farther west than Arkansas until I was almost a teenager, all such creatures and stories were but visions in a young man's dreams.

There was however one section of every issue that I always turned to first. *This Happened to Me* was a cartoon type feature that reenacted some disastrous event that had befallen some unfortunate outdoorsman. Whether it was an unwitting hunter stumbling upon a sow grizzly with cubs, or an errant fisherman who had fallen through the ice, most stories were cases of catastrophe and survival, events where a man had to really rely upon his skill, wits and more than a fundamental knowledge of the outdoors to come out alive. I think what attracted me to these articles the most was the fact that the proverbial "Me" could have been anyone, even myself! It brought the story and the message home to a very personal level. In every story the author managed to embed some realized truth from the event. The objective was to pass on a lesson learned to the reader in the hope that others would learn from the presented misfortune.

Such is the case in my story. While the triggering event may have been somewhat calamitous, and was surely an accident, the real gems are the lessons that were learned or reinforced as a result and along the way.

Lesson Learned #1: Murphy is Alive and Well…and Worthy of Your Respect.

The first of Murphy's Laws states, "If anything can go wrong, it will." Murphy's second law states that, "If there is a possibility of several things going wrong, the one that will cause the most damage [and bust your chops] will be the one to go wrong."

As a former United States Air Force aviator, a considerable part of our training consisted of planning for the unexpected. From day one in flight school we learned that every time we climbed into the cockpit, this invisible Murphy guy would climb in with us and go along for the ride. As a result, in all those years and thousands of hours in the cockpit, I never took a flight where I failed to prepare myself for the possibility of something going wrong. More so, even though I was a crewmember of a two-seat jet fighter, I never assumed that the other guy in the plane would be there to deal with whatever problem arose. I knew that if I had my stuff together and knew what procedures to follow, what courses of action were necessary, that I would be doing the most that I could to maximize my chances for survival as well as that of my fellow crewmember and the aircraft. I never depended upon the other guy to do it for me.

Lesson Learned #2: The Only Person Who Is Going to Lookout for You….Is You.

Elk hunting is fraught with all manner of potential risks, including surprise storms, the possibility of physical injury, or even becoming disoriented in an immense and unforgiving land. Research indicates that few hunters give would-be risks such as these any significant thought; even fewer consider what they would do in the event that something dire might happen. Such thoughts are usually placed far back in the mind frequently under the category of, "I'll deal with that later, if and when it ever happens," or "that only happens to other hunters." Plans are not in place, and contingencies for the unexpected are often not discussed with fellow hunters or family. In essence, when we fail to plan for the unforeseen, we are in fact planning to fail, and setting the stage for some future potential disaster. I was very fortunate in that my injuries, i.e. a severely dislocated shoulder, a torn rotator cuff, and a piece of bone tearing away from my shoulder, were relatively minor when compared to what could have happened. Well, let's get back to the story.

After Joe and I had gathered our wits, we began to analyze the situation that we were faced with. Almost immediately my Air Force survival training kicked in and I determined that we needed to come up with a course of action and we needed it quick. From the sun's low position on the horizon, I could tell that it would be getting dark (and much colder) soon. Both Joe and I had suffered what we suspected might be somewhat severe injuries leaving us in acute pain and somewhat debilitated. Joe was telling me that every time he took a breath his ribs shot fiery bolts throughout his body making it difficult for him to breathe and walk. My shoulder was so damaged that it racked me with some of the most intense pain I had ever known, making focusing on anything, much less a survival plan, that much more difficult.

As a part of my essential kit of "elk hunting stuff", I am rarely without my GPS. Currently I use what I believe to be one of the best GPS units on the market, my Magellan Explorist 500. Its 16-color display enables me to see where I am in vivid color. It has a high-speed USB data port and unlimited data storage capacity via secure digital (SD) card expandability, and I can easily add detailed topo maps from my Magellan MapSend® software.

However, on this one particular day, I had hastily decided to leave my GPS back at camp, since I knew that our guide relied on his GPS and always had it in his daypack. Wrong…Bad decision! Folks, never…ever leave camp without your GPS! In my desire to lighten my daypack load, I had broken one of my long time personal rules by choosing to rely on someone else for my own welfare while hunting.

With the sun getting lower by the minute, I knew that we had to get back to camp for help. Fortunately for us, over the course of five days of hunting, I had become acquainted with a few prominent landmarks. I also knew in general terms where our camp was in relationship to these. By visualizing our current position in relationship to these three landmarks, Joe and I were able to figure out the general direction that we would have to travel to get back to camp. Unfortunately, there was one problem that complicated our land navigation problem; neither of us was in any shape to handle the valleys and hills that lay along a straight-line path back to camp. Joe and I talked about it and decided that if we were to make it back to camp at all, we would have to keep to higher ground. This meant that we would have to travel a much longer and more roundabout route.

So off we went. Two banged-up hunters looking like something out of a rodeo wreck hobbling up a game trail at a pace that would make a snail look like Kurt Busch's #97 Nascar racer. I really have to give my hunting partner and friend Joe the lion's share of the credit. With a useless arm dangling towards the ground like a broken wing and having to walk like Quasimodo to minimize the pain, there was no way I could carry my backpack and its internal water supply. So Joe, fiery dinged up ribs and all, was the hero and volunteered to carry both of our packs. Thinking that going into shock was a possibility for either of us; we stopped regularly for water and to check up on each other for any signs of shock or dehydration.

I am a firm believer in the buddy system when it comes to hunting, especially in big country like the Colorado Rockies. **Tip:** Events like this are rock-solid arguments for never heading out into the backcountry alone.

After what seemed like three or four hours, but was in reality possibly just an hour or so, we came upon our guide and one of the other guides from camp riding toward us on the game trail with our wayward horses in tow. Two memories of this scene remain vividly etched in my recollection. First, not seeing anything resembling a look of remorse on the face of my horse, I really wanted to go over to him and give him a piece of my mind…or a bit more. Remember the scene in front of the saloon with Mongo and the horse in the movie Blazing Saddles? Second, I recall looking up at my horse and thinking to myself… NO WAY. So, in as cordial a way as I could think of, I promptly informed the young guide that there was no possible way for me to climb up on the horse with a busted up arm. More so, with my recent rodeo experience as fresh in my mind as an NFL Monday night replay, there was no way I was going to climb back up on any horse in the foreseeable future. I even recall that for a brief second, the image of a heavy-weight boxing champ hovering over his fallen opponent flashed through my mind, with his ominous words of warning echoing, "if you know what's good for you…you'll stay down too!"

Believing that my injuries were somewhat extensive and would require professional medical attention as soon as possible, and thinking that Joe might be in the same kind of shape or possibly even worse, I suggested that the guide hightail it back to camp and get on the cellular phone to the Search and Rescue folks and get a helicopter in the air. In response the young guide informed me, "You've probably just got a dislocated shoulder. I think I can probably fix that!" With all the willpower within me, I just thanked him for his offer and requested the helicopter again.

Lesson Learned # 3: Others may have good intentions …but in times like these sound judgment has to rule.

So Joe and I bowed our heads into the wind and once again stepped off on our trek up the ridge and on towards camp. Having to keep to the higher ground to avoid any significant climbing that neither of us could handle, our route took us on a fairly roundabout path back to camp, taking the better part of another hour.

When we finally reached camp, word of our misfortune had already gotten around. The camp cook to her credit had already placed the call that I requested to the outfitter's trailhead camp, which placed a follow-up call to the county Sheriff's office to initiate the rescue operation. I walked into camp on my own and made my way into our tent, where I tried to make myself as comfortable and stable as possible. By now my entire body was shaking uncontrollably. Whether this was from the adrenaline, shock, the cool outside temperature or a combination of all three I don't recall. I do remember that my biggest fears the entire time, and those that consumed most all of my thoughts was how to keep from going into shock, and how I was going to break this news to my new wife.

I am blessed with the most wonderful wife a guy could ever ask for. She loves me with all of her heart and encourages me daily to pursue my other loves, elk hunting and writing about elk hunting. Years ago, as a teenager, Rae Ann had lost her best friend in a horseback riding accident. Now after only a few months of marriage, this happens to me. I had to find a way to let her know about the accident while assuring her that I was in good hands and would be fine. I sent a message via the camp cook to the outfitter to hold off calling Rae Ann until I was onboard the helicopter and in the hands of trained medical professionals, thinking that would minimize her fears. Boy, do I have a lot to learn.

It is important to note that as I tell this story, I have no medical training beyond some basic level Red Cross and Air Force survival school first-aid courses. My recollection of what I knew about traumatic injury was that in many cases shock was a possibility, could be deadly, and should always be treated accordingly. In retrospect, I've learned that shock is usually caused by an abrupt loss of blood supply, which as it turned out was not the case. Nevertheless, I encourage anyone who plans to spend time in the backcountry to take a comprehensive course in first aid, so that if and when the time comes, you will have knowledge and skills necessary to render appropriate care. This is definitely an area where one must go beyond the fundamentals. Your life or that of someone you care about may depend on it.

Lesson Learned #4: Go beyond the basics and enroll in a comprehensive first aid course.

Time seemed to drag on forever as I lay there alone anticipating the sound of the rescue helicopter. There was virtually no position that I could assume that would relieve the nerve-wracking pain, which by now since the adrenaline had worn off was almost debilitating. That's right I was alone. I guess everyone got so caught up in preparing for the helicopter, that they forgot they had an injured party in camp. When one of the other hunters finally came into the tent, I asked him if he would mind checking on me from time to time. From that moment on, one of my fellow hunters was always there by my side. What a great bunch of guys. I owe every one of them a huge debt of gratitude.

Lesson Learned #5: Never leave an injured person alone if you are not sure of the extent of their injuries.

I had been laying there for what I thought was an hour or so when one of the other hunters, Spencer Ruff, who I had not had much chance to get to know walked in and asked how I was doing. I told him I was doing as well as possible given the circumstances, whereupon he came over and sat down on my cot and asked if he could pray for me. As a Christian, I am no stranger to prayer, having spent countless hours praying for others. But this was new, and even now as I write this, I am overcome with emotion as I relive the moment remembering the generosity, sensitivity, and Christian brotherly love of my newfound friend as he bowed his head and prayed to the one God of Heaven...for me.

Lesson Learned #6: There is nothing in heaven or on earth more prevailing than the power of prayer, especially when that prayer is emanating from an elk hunting buddy.

Just as the sun began to settle behind the purple mountains—yes they really are purple when the sun is just right—to the west, I heard the most welcomed sound I had heard all week, that of rotors tearing through the cold mountain air. I knew then that my ordeal was almost over and that I would be fine. With hunter orange vests volunteered from every hunter and guide in camp forming a make shift emergency landing zone, a Flight For Life helicopter carrying real angels of mercy landed just a few hundred yards from my tent. In no time a flight nurse and medical technician were beside me checking my vitals, and preparing me for the quickest trip out of the mountains I have ever had. In minutes we were airborne and on our way to a outstanding team of folks at Saint Mary's Hospital Emergency Room in Grand Junction, Colorado.

Post Story Update: As I write this, almost six months after the accident, I have just received an email from my 2004 hunting partner, Joe Novosel of Dutch Harbor, Alaska. Unknown to me or anyone else in camp at the time including Joe, the net result of Joe's encounter was far more damaging than anyone knew, i.e. three broken ribs. Count 'em folks...

three! Joe is as tough a guy as I have ever met, and no one hunts harder or longer than Joe did on our trip. Earlier I referred to Joe as a hero and that is exactly what he is, though he will likely argue the point when he reads this. Busted ribs and all, Joe hauled both sets of our gear all those miles back to camp...without a single complaint! I pray that I am never again in such circumstances, but should I be, I hope that I am fortunate enough to be hunting with Joe Novosel or a man like this true American hero. God bless you Joe. I will never forget you. Thank you!

Joe Novosel of Dutch Harbor, AK. Hunting partner - NW Colorado, 2004

Chapter Two

Where & How To Find Big Bulls

These days locating a mature bull can be like trying to track down a senior corporate executive when you have a problem with their company. Over the years they have become highly skilled at avoiding the public and go to great lengths to make sure that you cannot find them. Like executives, bulls are nonetheless creatures of habit and for the hunter who is committed to the task and determined to do what it takes to root them out, success is often a matter of time, hard work and patience.

The strategy that one uses to discover where the big boys are hiding to some extent will depend upon the season that you plan to hunt. Specifically, will you be hunting before, during or after the rut?

Good friend and a world class elk hunter Danny Farris's 2002 Bull, .300 Win. Mag

In most western elk hunting states, bowhunters and smoke-pole hunters (those who hunt with muzzleloaders) typically have a distinct advantage in this game as they are hunting pre-rut or during the rut. While bull elk are habitually cagey and elusive creatures throughout most of elk season, that annual rise of testosterone in bull elk associated with cow elk coming into estrus that encompasses what we call the rut, is a time where the bulls seem to set aide many of their rules of normal behavior. Let's take a moment to look at this phenomenon known as "the rut."

What Triggers the Commencement of the Rut?

Over the course of these many years of hunting elk, I have heard almost every imaginable theory for what stimulates bull elk to commence the rut. Some folks will tell you to subtract the number of days required for elk gestation from the actual calf drop date in a particular area in the previous year to determine when the rut will start, while others believe that the rut may be triggered by the position of the sun and moon in relation to the axis of the earth. Well, they may be right, who am I to argue? Needless to say, there are many theories about what causes the rut and the discussion of each and every one of these is far beyond the scope of this book.

In this writer's experience and that of a number of experts however, one explanation does seem to pass the test of holding water. Research indicates that the onset of the rut is directly related to the length of the day and the amount of available sunlight that passes through an elk's retina in a given time period. In response to the visual acquisition of a finite amount of sunlight, an elk's pituitary gland is neurologically stimulated to release hormones that produce testosterone, which then produces an urge in bull elk to begin their yearly courting ritual.   Having observed control situations conducted by wildlife biologists with whitetail deer in Texas some years ago, I agree that the amount of available light, and the frequency of the light/dark or day/night cycle does play a significant role in rut commencement as well as the antler shed cycle.

So when does the rut start some will ask? If I am hoping to time my hunt to hit within at least some portion of the rut, I look to the last two weeks of September. If your craving is for a more accurate prediction, then take a month of vacation, head out into your favorite part of elk country, set up camp…and wait. When you find out, please let me know. The point here being that elk hunting is not…I repeat NOT…an exact science. Heck, hunting is not science at all. Though for the life of me I cannot understand why so many try to make it so. Elk hunting is a lot of adventure, with a pinch of planning tossed in, a smidgen of luck, a bucket load of plain hard work, and a truckload of patience! So if you were looking for a formula that would increase your chances of putting an elk in the freezer, there it is… my best shot. If you apply this formula consistently, you will be far ahead of most of the other hunters you run into in elk country.

Bugling can be an excellent way to determine if a big bull is holed up deep in a canyon.
Danny Farris, Backcountry Bowhunt, 2004

Pre-Rut Hunt – Hunting Wallows

One of the best ways that I have found to successfully hunt big bulls in early September prior to the onset of the rut or even in the early stages of the rut is to search out elk country for wallows. Beginning in August, testy bulls will often start shredding the ground around a small seep or spring using their hooves and antlers. For weeks a bull will continue to repeat this process whipping the ground into perhaps the biggest, nastiest mud hole you've ever seen. Big bulls often lower their head and urinate all over the dark mane on the underside of their neck. Whew, can you believe that? And then... he'll go and roll around in the wallow like a sow hog that's just had a hot date with a big ol' boar. This behavior, as nasty as it may seem, serves two very authentic purposes. First the scent of the urine soaked hair makes the bull smell like Romeo to cows, which think of themselves as Juliet that will soon come into estrus. Second, when this ol' boy rolls in the mud, some of the scent is transferred to the wallow thereby marking this bull's territory to other bulls as well as cows. In a short time these wallows will acquire an awfully distinctive and musky odor that is easily identifiable as elk and can be detected by hunters at some distance. Take it from me folks; once you get a snoot full of this… you will never forget the smell.

A frequently used wallow can be a hunter's dream. Andy Farris, 2004

A second source of odor that is sometimes transferred to the wallow is from the bull's preorbital glands. Preorbital glands are seen as the deep dark folds in front of and below the eye. These contain a thick waxy material that also is distinctly odorous. When a bull bugles he opens his preorbital glands, which in turn release this odor. The more he bugles; the more of his scent is released into the air.

Well, what's a wallow look like? Wallows may be only a few feet in diameter or they can be ten feet or more across. There are even stories of wallows becoming so deep and extensive as to virtually swallow a wayward elk entirely should he stray into it. If you happen across a torn up wet spot in the course of your scouting or your hunt, take a whiff. Does that musky bouquet smell familiar? If it is an active wallow, there will be no mistaking the smell.

After a big bull takes his turn in the "tub", you can bet that he is fairly full of himself — frisky one might say — and often he takes out his chemically induced aggression on the flora and fauna surrounding the wallow. After tearing up a tree or small sapling, a bull may rub the area of his face near the preorbital gland on the tree, thus transferring his scent or mark. Look for torn up bushes or rubs on small saplings. If it is a well-used wallow, there should be an abundance of sign in the immediate area. To put it more clearly, he may have torn up everything in sight!

Prior to the rut, a bull will come back to the same wallow over and over. Actually some bulls have been known to return to the same wallow, year after year. If you find such a wallow in the course of your excursions into elk country, file this gem away in your notebook. This is a spot you will want to revisit next season.

Bulls often rub small saplings like this one to mark their territory
and help remove the velvet from their antlers. Danny Farris, 2004

How can you tell if a wallow was used recently? If it's been a while since anyone has come to call, the top edges of the tracks will be rounded off and the track may contain debris. If the tracks are crisp with little water in them, then you can figure a bull may have visited the wallow within the past few hours. If you can reach down with great care and gently touch the water or mud just in the center of the wallow with the tip of your index finger and if it is slightly warm to the touch, I think such would be an opportune time to knock an arrow or remove the safety on your rifle. Sorry about that, I just couldn't help myself. Sometimes writers just get carried away.

In some cases more than one bull may use a wallow. While this doesn't happen often, if and when both show up at the same time, this can make for an interesting photographic moment. If you're an early season bowhunter or smoke-pole shooter consider hunting the wallows. If you are a long-time whitetail hunter accustomed to hunting from a tree stand, this may be as close as you get to successfully hunting elk from such a stand.

Hunting the Rut

While bachelor groups appear almost sedate during the summer months when many of us are a field on scouting trips, laying around in meadows taking in the sun, everything changes when the air starts to chill, the days start getting shorter, and the Aspen begin their yearly transformation from green to gold.

Throughout most of the hunting season a bull elk is as skittish as a long-tailed cat in a room full of rockin' chairs. With the unwelcome assault of thousands of smelly hunters into their backyard, bulls are tempted to quickly head out for their favorite hides.

A late summer group of bachelor bulls still in velvet.

Fortunately for us elk hunters, Mother Nature has thrown a curve into the elk's plan in the form of rising testosterone and the need to breed. I guess one could look at bull elk as young and foolish fighter pilots like in the movie Top Gun walking around a bar, thinking something like, "I have the need...the need to breed." And just like that cocky aviator, a bull elk lets something other than his better judgment override his natural instincts for survival. If you want to hunt elk at their most "at risk" time, the rut is by far the best time to go hard and heavy after big bulls.

Hunting the rut can be one of the most exhilarating events in the life of an elk hunter. If for no other reason, it is that time of the year when the clear crisp Ooh-h-h-e-e-e-E-E-E-a-h-h bugle of a bull elk slices through a frosty September morning like a hot knife through butter. Streams that ran freely throughout the summer begin to form thin layers of ice while colors of red and gold seem to burst from every avenue of the high country.

The nerve-tingling bugle of bull elk in September is what makes hunting the rut one of the most exciting and memorable adventures one will ever experience.

One of the most memorable of these mornings was a few years back. Mike Byrd and I were hunting a deep gulch west of Rocky Mountain National Park. I was set up on a steep fir covered hillside overlooking a well-used game trail and doing a rather poor job of keeping warm. My watch told me that sunrise was not far off, but you could have fooled me. It was darker than a well digger's belt buckle. I was facing due east and there was not a shred of light to be seen in any direction. As I shifted my position trying to burrow myself into the hillside in the hope that some measure of warmth might be hidden beneath the pine needles on the forest floor, a slow and low-pitched growl issued forth from the valley floor below, gradually building, growing higher and higher until I thought that whatever manner of beast that had made it would surely bust a gut before it was all over. As the bugle hit what I thought would be its high note, another began and then another until it seemed as if the entire valley had become some sort of natural orchestra. I must admit that in all of my years hunting, I have never before and have not since been witness to a more beautiful symphony. The bugling went on, non-stop, for what seemed like half an hour. Much of the time, I simply sat and listened with my eyes closed imaging the elk singing to one another. When at last the orchestra ceased, I opened my eyes and behold the eastern sky had turned away from the dark of night ushering in another day as if the sun was called to rise up by the elk themselves. Wow! Now that is what elk country is all about.

The serenade of big bull elk bugling has become synonymous with the rut. So why do bulls bugle? Evidence suggests that the primary reason bulls bugle is to attract cows. In the mating ritual it is the cow that makes the decision which bull she will mate with. Knowing that the survival of her calf will depend to a great extent upon its genetic makeup, the cow seeks a mate that will be able to pass along those desirable traits that she is looking for, 6'3", opaline green eyes, dark wavy hair…. just joking folks. Really, the choices that determine the future viability and vitality of the herd are made by the cow, so she will seek out the most robust and healthy bull that she can find to mate with. Larger more dominant bulls tend to produce a deeper more aggressive bugle. Cows know this and are attracted to these genetically superior bulls.

Larger more dominant bull elk like this one produce a deeper more aggressive sounding bugle.

When a bull bugles he will extend his neck and raise his head tilting his chin upward opening his mouth often curling his upper lip back exposing his top row of teeth including his upper incisors or buglers, sometimes referred to as ivories. From deep within his massive chest the bull begins to exhale, the hot air rushing upwards through his trachea, across his vocal cords and outwards across his retracted tongue into the air. As he exhales more and more pressure is exerted on the diaphragm causing the airflow to quicken. It is by controlling the airflow that the bull changes the pitch of the sounds coming forth.

When a rutting bull has gathered his cows his bugle is often lower and shorter sounding more like E E E eunk...eunk, eunk. It is a brief series of guttural grunts designed to console his cows, settle them down and strengthen the bond with them that he has established. This is far different from the full-blown three-octave bugle, designed to ward off other bulls saying, "Stay away. These girls are mine. If you know what's good for you, you'll leave now."

If you have a bugle and know how to use it, the rut is the one time, in my opinion, that this type of a call can make a very real and positive difference in the outcome of your hunt, as bulls are more susceptible to calling at this time. Once the rut has passed, I usually put my pack bugle in the bottom of my daypack and leave it there. Experience has demonstrated that once the breeding season is nearly done, a bugle tends to get the elk's attention all right; it pushes them into the next county. The last thing a bull that has been herding and breeding cows for weeks needs is to get into it with another bull. More often than not they are prone to just gather the girls up and head out at the first sight or sound of another bull.

This bull is testing one of his cows to determine if she has come into estrus or not. A cow's estrus cycle may only last a few hours, so it is important for the herd bull to keep tabs on things.

The estrus cycle in cow elk is quite brief lasting only a few hours in some cases. As cows begin to come into estrus, the bull is continually checking out his cows to determine which are ready to breed. He does this by following the cow closely using his highly tuned nose and tongue to detect the change in the smell of her urine. If the bull thinks that the cow is nearing the beginning of her cycle he will lick her genital area to incite the cow to urinate so that he can better determine if she is ready to mate. Special receptors in a bull elk's mouth tell him if she is in estrus.

The actual act of mating in elk is fast and furious lasting only seconds. A bull will mount a cow grasping her sides just forward of her rear legs with his front legs. He immediately thrust his pelvis and penis often making a loud shrieking type sound. The act itself is over almost before it begins and the bull moves on to another cow.

Kevin Fair's 6 x 5 Bull, North Central Colorado, 2004, .300 WSM

Post-Rut Hunt

It's October in the high country, and the Aspen have shed their leaves of gold leaving the grove floors covered with a layer of dry crackling leaves that make a stealthy stalk a real challenge even for the most experienced of hunters. Breeding has for the most part run its course with the exception of late season cows and the bulls while they may still be herded up with a little romance on their mind are dead-tired and starting to think of transitioning back into their more solitary lifestyle. They know that the coming winter with its lack of forage is just around the corner and that they must try to pack in as many calories as possible before the deep snows come. Post rut is the time of the rifleman.

The Morning Hunt

Elk are nocturnal creatures, feeding primarily at night they begin their journey back to their bedding areas before or at the latest soon after daybreak. If you want to get into the elk, you will need to have spent some preseason time scouting out these transition routes that the elk use to move from their feeding areas to their bedding areas, and plan to be in a place to set an ambush well before daylight. Don't show up on Friday afternoon before the season opener on Saturday and expect to locate and pattern the elk in your area. This is especially true if you are not hunting the first season of the year. Once hunters have begun to invade elk country the elk will feel the pressure and react accordingly. It doesn't take but a few days of archery season, which is usually the first season of the year, for the elk to adjust their travel routes to avoid confrontation with hunters. Summer scouting trips are invaluable in helping a hunter to learn how to navigate an area and determine if in fact elk in huntable numbers inhabit the ground. But elk will adjust their patterns once they determine that a threat exists. Have you ever wondered why on the days before the opener of the first elk season you saw elk all over the place and the morning of opening day, there were no elk to be found...anywhere? Well...Duh! How about a zillion stinking hunters "scouting" out a good stand on the day before season opens? For more on early morning tactics you may want to read my first book, *Elk Hunting 101, A Pocketbook Guide to Elk Hunting.*

As much as I hate to say this there are only two ways to get there ahead of the elk in the morning hours, you have to either leave camp two to three hours before daylight, emphasis on "leave camp" not set the alarm to go off, depending upon how long it will take you to walk into your stand, or you will need to get there the day before and set up a spike camp and stay the night. My good friend and hunting partner Roger Medley shares some thoughts about this option later in the book in the chapter on backcountry bowhunting. While Roger's discussion is directed to bowhunters, the argument of the value of a spike camp that allows the hunter to remain near the elk applies to rifle hunters as well.

The Midday Hunt

As more and more hunters have made their way into elk country, the elk have retreated. Originally elk were plains animals, but when man began to expand civilization in America westward the elk sought refuge where they could find it, in the high country of the Rockies. Today with civilization encroaching on elk habitat in the form of 35-acre ranchetts, condos, and freeways from every direction, the elk have again adapted and moved deeper and deeper into the dark timber for security and survival.

The process of digestion for elk takes considerable time so after feeding throughout the night, the elk retire to the refuge of dark timber where they can rest and ruminate or digest. If the elk can find water, security, and relief from the heat and bugs in the timber, they will stay there throughout the majority of the middle of the day, only occasionally wandering out to the fringes. If you want to find elk during the middle of the day or between roughly 9:00 a.m. and 3:00 p.m. then you will have to gear up to head into the dark stuff to find them. Here is where a first-rate set of binoculars can come in handy in helping to locate big bulls before they locate you. Before you go crashing over deadfalls, a thorough glassing of the area is called for. Good optics with low-light capability can make the difference between success and failure. Take time to use your optics to search out every possible place a bull could hide. Look for low horizontal lines that may be the back of a bull. This is no time to get in a hurry. Look for a patch of light color in the midst of the green foliage or the glint off of the tip of an antler. Depending upon the distances involved, you may not be able to pick up these details without the aid of your binoculars. For dense searches in dark timber I'm never without my Alpen Apex 10 X 42 binoculars. Weighing in at a modest 24 ounces with an impressive 315 F.O.V (ft@1000yds.), and providing crisp optical clarity in the most adverse of conditions they are second to none in my book.

How do you know if you are in good elk country in the middle of the day? If you cannot take two steps without having to crawl over or under something, if you get whacked in the head with a branch a couple of times a minute, if your workload has tripled from that you experienced while hunting open meadows and you want to turn around and call it a day, if you say to yourself I could never pack an elk out of this mess then you are probably in good elk territory. Press on.

It's hard work but hunting dark timber can be one of your best midday bets.

Successful elk hunters are those who are willing to endure all of this abuse and more. They are what I call the ten-percenters, meaning that ninety percent of the hunters that encounter this type of hunting area will quit. Most will never attempt to penetrate what could be the most productive areas because of the difficulty of the hunting conditions. I have said it before so I'll say it again. Elk hunting is hard work and to consistently be successful it requires a level of commitment well beyond what the average hunter is willing to make. That is why the success ratios hover only in the ten to fifteen percent range. If you want to be more successful at elk hunting, you have to make the commitment.

Hunting dark timber during midday requires stealth and a keen awareness of the wind. If elk have adequate water and security, they will bed in the same general area day after day unless they are disturbed. Just like you know the layout of your own home and especially your bedroom like the back of your hand, the elk are familiar with their bedding areas as well and quick to pick up on any changes. If you want to sneak up on elk during midday you will have to be on your toes. I used to carry a small talc squeeze bottle with me to determine wind direction, but have since changed my method of determining wind direction to a small disposable lighter. A quick flick of the lighter gives me an instant read on the wind direction. If in the course of a stalk the flame from the lighter indicates that the wind has shifted in favor of the elk, I will wait a minute or so to make sure that it wasn't just a momentary swirl. If a second test tells me the wind is from my back, I am outta there! No matter how much work I may have done to get to that point, there is no point moving forward with an unfavorable wind. I will back out of the area as quietly as I came in and attempt to approach it from another direction. An elk's primary sense of detecting danger is its nose and if the wind is coming from your back, you are wasting your time by continuing the stalk. To emphasize this point, I have seen a herd of elk react to my human scent while glassing them on a slope over a mile away. I was scoping the herd through my spotting scope and everything is going great and the elk are content grazing but then all you-know-what breaks loose.

The sentry cow determines whether the herd stays put or heads out when trouble is detected. If she busts you, it's probably all over.

Normally the first to detect danger in the herd is the lead or sentry cow. She can be recognized as a large, older, more rotund looking cow whose head and neck is continually coming up sniffing the air, with ears always on a swivel. Depending upon how much of a snoot full of you she gets and how significant she perceives the threat to be, she may just increase her alert status and monitor the situation. Other cows beginning to stand up and mill around with a higher state of anxiety than before often evidence this. The younger cows are always watching the lead cow, so if she gets nervous, they get nervous. Or she may begin a slow walk or trot in the opposite direction. Worst case she may issue an alarm bark and haul buns over the mountain taking the herd with her. What happened? The wind busted you.

The Evening Hunt

The last thirty minutes before dark can be some of the best time of the day to hunt elk. As the sun retreats over the ridgelines into the west, the elk begin to drift out of the fringes of the timber where they have spent most of the day and begin their trek toward their feeding areas. This is not, emphasis on not, the time to be walking back to camp because you don't want to get caught out after dark. An evening hunt near a frequently used water source such as a spring or small creek can often be very productive. Elk love to feed on the sweet succulents found alongside streams and seeps where moisture is abundant. If you can locate such a water source in close proximity to a small hidden meadow where dark timber closes in on one or more sides you may have found a good spot to set up.

The timing of when the elk will move out of their bedding areas in the dark timber towards the area in which they plan to feed can depend upon a number of factors. If hunter pressure has been heavy or if the weather has been unseasonable warm, the elk may chose to remain in the shelter of the timber until well after dark leaving the hunter little or no opportunity. Consider these as you plan your next evening hunt, but by all means, do not give up and head back to camp until it is too dark to make a safe shot or legal hunting hours have expired.

Marc Smith of Colorado Springs, a first-rate bowhunter
with his heavy-beamed 6 x 6 bull. SW Colorado, 2004

Chapter Three

Extreme Elk Hunting For Big Bulls

As recently as fifteen years ago bull elk regularly responded enthusiastically and repeatedly to the challenge of the hunter's bugle. Whether the hunter issued his challenge by mimicking a mature bull trying to pick a fight with the herd bull or just as a smaller satellite bull trying to entice a few cows his way, the result was almost always the same, an instant and assertive reply by the dominant bull to clear out or look out.

Today things have changed. While the elk themselves may not have changed much over the years, the environment in which we pursue them has altered dramatically. Much of twenty first century elk country is literally overrun with hunters, ATV's, mountain bikes, backpackers, woodcutters, bird watchers, and my favorite...ranchetts. The net result is more pressure on the elk than possibly at any other point in history. In addition, in many areas the age class of bull elk overseeing herds is getting younger and younger. The number of older more experienced bulls in many areas is just not what it used to be. In the seventies the number of elk harvested in a given year where I live in Colorado have been in the neighborhood of 10,000 animals. According to the Colorado Division of Wildlife, during the 2004 elk-hunting season over 61,000 elk were harvested.

Mature herd bull keeping close watch. North Central, Colorado, 2004

Not too many years ago the average herd bull was in the six to seven-year-old bracket. Having survived many hunting seasons and harsh winters these bulls had the experience to know how to react when the hunting pressure increased. Today it is not unusual to find three year old bulls controlling a herd. Why? Because the number of older more experienced bulls just isn't what it used to be. Just one year ago, this bull was running at the slightest provocation or advance from another bull. Now as a wet-behind-the-ears, untried two-year-old, he has his own harem. So what does he do when challenged by a hunter's bugle? Lacking any significant measure of experience, he flees and takes the herd with him. Now what can hunters do differently to compensate for this type of behavior?

Immature herd bull, North Central, Colorado, 2004

It is my conviction that all creatures, including man, have as a part of their innate composition a fight or flight mechanism that involuntarily engages the brain and the rest of the body to action whenever certain conditions are present. Extreme Elk Hunting™ is about forcing a bull into a fight response instead of a flight response.

For as long as I can recall conventional elk hunting strategy has revolved around such tactics as stealth, deception, calling, scent containment, and a few more. The prudent hunter would do his homework learning where the elk live, arise early, and put on clothing that would not only break up his human form but possibly mask his scent as well. He would quietly make his way to his pre-scouted point of ambush, pull out his call and begin the process of trying to lure a nice bull to within rifle or bow range. In many cases this strategy would bless the hunter with a good supply of meat in the freezer for the coming winter.

However, in more situations than many of us want to admit, the hunter just cannot close the deal and get the bull to come in. Try as he may, the bull hangs up out of range or upon hearing the hunter's lure in the form of a bugle or cow call, he takes his harem in the other direction and hope of meat in the freezer is lost.

There is another tactic that has proven itself in situations like the one described above that I like to call Extreme Elk Hunting. Extreme elk hunting is an "in your face" approach that is designed to place the hunter inside a bull's comfort zone and provoke a desired response. To visualize what I mean, let me draw you a picture that you may be familiar with.

Two guys are having a conversation about some subject that each is rather passionate about. The conversation starts out at normal voice levels, but as the dialogue continues each person becomes more and more insistent that his point of view is the right point of view. At this point either is still in a position to choose to step away or flee from the confrontation. Soon voices are raised and the two move closer to one another exhibiting a heightened state of anxiety and aggression. Now the option to back off is being overridden by one or both person's fight or flight mechanism with the fight option taking the upper hand. As the confrontation continues to escalate, one of the guys decides to put his finger in the other guy's chest to make his point. Now things are really heating up. Not only has the guy with the finger taken the flight option away from what has now become his opponent, he has crossed the line into the other fellow's personal space. Depending upon one's ability to deal with aggression and conflict it is just a matter of time before something blows. The finger guy continues to poke the other guy in the chest when all of a sudden all control is lost and the fellow on the receiving end of the finger explodes. Inhibitions, better judgment, self-preservation, and a host of other societal conditioning responses are thrown out the window. The bull …I mean the man comes looking for a fight!

This is what I mean by Extreme Elk Hunting tactics. Rather than leaving the bull with an option to flee, the hunter moves in aggressively attempting to get inside the bull's comfort zone. Once you have closed inside of 100 yards or so, it's time to pick a fight. But before you put your finger in his chest here are a few more factors to consider.

As you know, wind is more stable and blows primarily down slope in the early morning hours. This is the best time for Extreme Elk Hunting. As the day warms, wind currents will start to swirl and become very unpredictable. For such Extreme Elk Hunting tactics to work, the hunter must be able to determine wind direction and depend on it to remain fairly consistent for a period of time. Once the wind direction has been determined you will want to plan a route that will take you to the bull with a favorable wind. This may mean that you will have to plan a circular attack, circling the side or even behind the bull to approach him with the wind in your face. Never forget that an elk's primary means of detecting danger is his nose. Wind is critical to your success. Never assume that because you cannot smell yourself that the elk cannot smell you. An elk's sense of smell is hundreds of times more sensitive than that of any human. If you cannot achieve a stalk with a favorable wind, back off and wait for a more favorable opportunity.

Kenny Medley, sets up for a close "in your face" shot. South Central Colorado

Next you will want to choose a setup that offers you an option of clear shooting lanes and cover. This is critical because once you stir your bull up there is a good chance that he will come in fast and mad, and he may come in without making a sound. You will need to be able to react quickly. Unlike long-range hunting where you may cow call or bugle to the bull from a quarter of a mile away and have time to pick and choose how you want the encounter to happen, Extreme Elk Hunting tactics can force the encounter and hopefully the shot in a matter of seconds. If your bull is bugling, try to get a fix on him as you move in. You may have determined his location earlier by glassing him, but he may move as you press your attack. If you use your bugle to locate the bull, redirect your calls using a grunt tube pointed back towards your original location, so that he will not have detected that you are closing the gap on him.

Now you are inside the bull's comfort zone. The wind is in your favor, you have chosen the best setup that you can by predicting how you think the bull will move in on you. You have identified shooting lanes that will provide you with clear shots. It is time to start the fight. Pull out your bugle making sure to again redirect the call back in the direction from which you came because that is where the bull expects you to be and sound off. This is the time to be as aggressive as you can be. If you had another option to be less aggressive, or seductive you would have tried these already. In essence like the example you are now standing in front of your opponent—think of him this way—you are in his face and it is time for both of you to put up or shut up. Give him your best, "I want a piece of you" bugle, which is basically putting your finger in his chest, knock your arrow or ready your rifle and get ready to rumble.

By making your stealth stalk you will have slipped into the bull's comfort zone. When you bugle it may take him a second to put two and two together and figure out what just happened. More than likely he will be startled as he thought you were still over on the other ridge. Now you are in his face. If you have worked this right, there is a very good chance that the bull will come straight in on you. He may respond to your challenge with a scream of his own. If your bull is inside of 100 yards my recommendation is if you think he is moving towards you be quiet and prepare for the shot. Bulls are squirrelly with minds of their own, so be ready for him to come in however he wants. If he does not come to you via one of your shooting lanes be ready to shift your position using cover and concealment to get into a better position for a shot.

That's it folks, the quick and dirty on Extreme Elk Hunting. Every elk hunter needs to have a few tricks in his pocket for those times when conventional methods of elk hunting are just not getting the job done. Extreme Elk Hunting is just such a hip pocket option. It is not for every situation, but it just may be the trick you need to put that special bull that won't come to the call over the mantel.

Here are two quick stories of where what I will call Ultra Extreme Hunting tactics closed the deal when nothing else would work. Don't try these at home folks.

I witnessed the first via a video of a young hunter who was after a grizzly with a long bow. The camera is at a safe distance behind the hunter who sees his target, this monster grizzly making its way along the edge of a meadow heading towards an Alder patch. There is absolutely no cover between him and the bear taller than six inches. The hunter knows that if the bear makes it into the Alder patch that all will be lost so he must take the bear before it gets into the Alders in the wide open meadow. So what does this kid do? You are not going to believe this. He charges the bear. Running full tilt on an intercept across this wide-open meadow in plain view of the bear he runs straight towards what appears to be about 800 pounds of teeth and claws. At what appears from the camera's point of view to be about twenty yards from the bruin, the hunter throws on the skids, draws his bow and looses an arrow. Folks I was just watching the video and my heart was about to stop. I cannot imagine what may have been going through the hunter's mind at this point. Well get this, the bear goes down like he was hit in the head by a bolt of lightning. Down, no movement, no nothing! Talk about taking the fight to the animal! Once everyone was sure the freight train size critter was down for good, they approach the now expired grizzly and witnessed what took the bear down so fast. The bowhunter had perfectly placed his arrow through the bear's right eye and buried half the shaft in the bear's brain. Folks I do not know whether this shot placement was intentional or not. That was not discernable from the video. More so I would not by any stretch of the imagination recommend that anyone take such a risk...especially with something that can eat you. The point however is that in some circumstances Extreme Hunting tactics may be called for and the hunter should have a few of these stashed away for such a time.

Very briefly, the second story was a very similar situation except the target was a bull elk. The hunter could find no alternative other than to charge the bull full speed across a meadow. Stopping about twenty yards from the bull, the hunter loosed the fateful arrow bringing his hunt and the future of this particular bull elk to a close. This is another example of where Extreme Elk Hunting tactics can make the difference between success, and going home empty-handed.

Chapter Four

Six Reasons Elk Hunters Go Home Empty Handed

A few years back, a good friend and in my opinion world-class hunter Steve Chapman wrote a fine book entitled *What a Hunter Brings Home*. In this volume like so many of his before it, Steve captures the joy of the hunt and demonstrates how God uses the solitude of the woods to reveal His eternal truths. Not too long ago, I was talking with a mutual friend of mine and Steve's, Lindsey Williams of Really Big Bison Productions of Nashville, when Lindz shared with me the story of the day he brought home his copy of Steve's book.

According to Lindz, he walked into the house and rather innocently said to his wife Susan "Honey, look what Steve gave me, a copy of his book, *What a Hunter Brings Home*."

Now I imagine that to get the total effect of this heart rending moment, we would have had to be there, but I bet most of us can get the picture. Being the faithful and loving wife of such a devoted husband and die-hard hunter, Susan merely replied, "Yeah...nuthin'!"

I don't know about the rest of you folks, but for me and a lot of folks I know this response is probably far more accurate than most of us want to admit. As elk hunters we spend countless days and a fair portion of the family budget in pursuit of game, only to return home bone-tired, smelly, cold, and worst of all, empty-handed. So let's spend a few minutes looking at six reasons why elk hunters go home with empty coolers.

Reason #1...Lack of A Good Plan or Not Following the Plan

Some things are worth repeating. In *Elk Hunting 101* I talked about doing your homework. This means that if you want to be more successful in your elk hunting endeavors, then you need to do a moderate amount of research into such things as: Where are the elk? How is your hunting party going to attack the problem of covering every inch of that area? And how are you going to manage the tags within your group? As you know, I love to tell stories that make a point. Here's one such story.

A few years ago my hunting partner and I took a whole bunch of guys with us elk hunting. No you don't want to know how many. Just take my word for it. It was a real gaggle. Our original thinking at the time was the more the merrier. Hindsight being 20/20, it is perfectly clear now that our ElkCamp for that year probably resembled more of a goat rope with an awful lot of effort going on, but little in the way of results coming from it. As in most camps old hunting friends chose to pair up and take to the woods in teams. I have no problem with such strategies. I do it myself. One of the most rewarding aspects of elk hunting is the hours of camaraderie spent with good friends in pursuit of a wild and worthy adversary.

In this particular camp our number of bull tags and cow tags were about equal. So far so good, right? Well yes and no. One would think that having a fair number of either type tag would be an overall smart plan. I agree it was. However, as our hunters partnered up each day to head out, guess how those tags were distributed? Let me tell you. About three-quarters of our hunters disregarded the type of tag their hunting partner had and we ended up with a bunch of cow tags going one way and a bunch of bull tags heading another. You can see this coming, can't you? Yep. The guys with bull tags ran into cows and the hunters with cow tags ran into bulls with neither having a legal opportunity to take a shot. On the next to the last morning of our hunt, two of our cow tag hunters walked up on two very nice shooter bulls. One was a large 6x6 and the other a very respectable 5x5. The 5x5 was broadside in the open at about sixty yards and the 6x6 was around 200 yards. Although these two hunters came back to camp with a great story and life-long memory of the hunt, such stories are not quite as tasty as elk tenderloin, which might have been the case if at least one of the hunters had a bull tag.

Big bulls like this 6 x 6 are few and far between. Be prepared.

Whether you are part of a college football team, an armored cavalry unit, or a just a bunch of guys going elk hunting, if you want to defeat your adversary, if you want to survive, if you want to be successful, you have to have a plan to succeed and you must work that plan. Otherwise what may happen is chaos and you end up going home often enough empty handed.

Reason #2…Poor Physical Condition

I am going to hazard a guess that many who read this are parents. If you're not in this category, then try to remember back to when you were a child. As a parent, how many times did you have to tell your child "no" after he or she continued to repeat the same infraction over and over. Reason leads one to believe that once should be enough. However, reality tells us that this just isn't the case. Some kids…some folks just need to hear it more than once.

Elk hunting is hard work. Let me say this again. Elk hunting is hard work! Some of those factors that come into play in the course of a day of hunting such as weather or terrain are finite. By this I mean that there is not much that you can do to change these. The mountains are always going to be brutal on your lungs and your knees. The wind and the cold are forever going to be obstacles that we have to deal with. These are all a part of what we sign on for as elk hunters. There are factors that can become obstacles only if we allow them to become so.

Fine physical specimens from our 2003 Elk Camp at 12,000 feet. Where did all the air go?
(L-R) Jay Houston, Steve Chapman, Emmitt Beall, Larry Money, & Roger Medley.
South Central Colorado, 2003

To enjoy the adventure of elk hunting one does not have to become the equivalent of an Olympic athlete. One does however need to be in reasonably good physical shape. This means that whether you are thirty or fifty, you should make a reasonable attempt to be prepared to hike from five to as much as fifteen miles a day with all of your gear. It means that if you want to get into elk, you have to be able and willing to do more than walk a quarter mile from the truck and sit down and hope an elk stumbles by you. If you want to be successful at elk hunting you have to be able to go where the elk are, so take the time before your hunt to get into shape.

Reason # 3…Hunting Where There Are No Elk

You can have the best strategy and the hottest new gear, but if you're not hunting where the elk are, well…it sort of becomes a moot point, doesn't it? Elk, being creatures of habit, opportunity, and need, are predictable as long as there are no external factors stirring up their day-to-day routine. By external factors I mean predators, particularly the two-legged gun-toting variety. Similar to human infants whose daily schedule is overly simplistic: eat…sleep…poop…eat…sleep… the routine of the elk is fairly straight forward as well revolving around what and where they eat.

Throughout the long days of summer the elk are content to graze on the sweet green grasses found in abundance just below timberline and on high ridges. But as the days become noticeably shorter and summer fades into fall, nighttime temperatures drop below freezing and nature begins to shut off the nutrients that had supplied the grasses in the high country throughout the summer, quite quickly the elk begin to notice the difference in the quality of their food supply. What was sweet and yummy just a few weeks ago is now becoming far less attractive to the elk's palate, much like a bag of store bought salad that has been opened and left in the refrigerator too long. Consequently in early autumn the elk will often move down the mountain to lower elevations where the graze has yet to be affected by the colder temperatures.

Evidence of such transitions can be witnessed by its affect on agriculture at these lower elevations. Alfalfa fields are favorites for elk. Unlike other grasses, which die off rather quickly after the first frosts, alfalfa will remain green for weeks and the elk know this. Once the elk locate a good patch of alfalfa they have been known to travel miles to get at it, feeding throughout the night and heading back up the mountain before daylight.

Another way to determine if the elk have moved down low is to check the status of ranchers' haystacks in the area. Haystacks can be a prime source of elk feed. Once hay is cut, bailed and stacked, it doesn't take long for the outer layers of the bails to turn brown. A quick scouting trip around your hunting area to see if any of the haystacks have been worked over by elk leaving the fresh greenish yellow hay beneath the outer layer visible can be a clue as to where the elk might be, or at least where they are feeding.

Once the frost line begins to move down the mountain and the lowlands' graze begins to lose its appeal, the elk will usually move back up the mountain to feed as the grasses up high have now cured and become attractive nourishment again.

In drought years water sources can also be an excellent place to find elk. Find the water and you will find the elk. If the high country has had plenty of rain or the snow pack from the previous winter has left streams with water in them, this tactic doesn't work as well.

After feeding throughout the night, the elk will begin making their way back up the mountain to their bedding areas in the timber before sunrise. A smart hunter will try and get to elk camp three to four days ahead of the season and spend time glassing the area in the early morning and late evening hours to locate the travel routes that the elk are using to move back and forth between their feeding areas and their bedding areas.

Glassing and Optics

While we are on the subject of glassing I think a brief discussion on the need for quality optics is in order. For scouting, nothing beats a good spotting scope and tripod. Binoculars are excellent for glassing during the hunt, but when glassing for prolonged periods, a spotting scope on a tripod will significantly reduce the physical effort on the hunter, and the higher levels of magnification often will help the hunter to spot and classify that far off bull that might not be as visible with binoculars.

Factors to consider when purchasing a spotting scope include: How will you be using the scope? Will you be glassing slopes from your vehicle on a road, or will you be packing the scope into the backcountry? If so, how much weight can you afford to add to your pack? How much do you have in your budget? In *Elk Hunting 101* I made the statement "Don't go cheap on optics. Buy the best optics that you can afford." As one spends more, the general rule is that you get a higher quality and often a lighter weight optical product for a given magnification capacity. Unless you have an unlimited budget, there will however come a point where you have to ask yourself, what is the best that I can buy without breaking the bank and incurring the wrath of my family? Over the years I have tried optics, i.e. binoculars and spotting scopes from one end of the spectrum to the other and have concluded that I do not have to spend the kid's college education money to acquire good optics. Alpen Optics of Rancho Cucamonga, CA, a relatively new player on the sports optics scene (1997) produces what I believe are absolutely first-class optics at a very affordable price. Key criteria that I look for when purchasing optics are: clarity at all light levels with an exit pupil of 4-5 mm, weather-proof, light-weight (24-28 oz. for binoculars and 25-30 oz. for spotting scopes), shock-resistant, fully multi-coated lenses to prevent the glass surfaces from reflecting or losing light, and a longer eye relief because I wear glasses. My optics setup includes two spotting scopes: a high-power variable magnification scope for glassing very long distances from roads, Alpen Model 788 20-60X80 with a 45 degree eyepiece, and an Alpen Model 730 15-30X50 scope for packing to camp.

As you can see, I have become a one-manufacturer kind of guy. The reason, when I find a great product supported by a team of professionals at an affordable price, I go for it.

If a spotting scope is not in the budget this year, then consider upgrading your binoculars. For years I have hunted day in and day out with 10X42 roof prism binoculars. My Alpen Apex Model 495 is the perfect all around elk hunting binocular. Recently however, as my eyesight has changed with age, and because there are times when I just don't want the extra bulk of a spotting scope in my daypack, I have added a set of Alpen Apex Model 499 12X50 binoculars to my gear, to be used in lieu of the spotting scope for pack-in type hunts. At first I was skeptical of using a single set of such powerful binoculars thinking that the narrower field of view trade-off for that extra magnification would not be worthwhile. Was I wrong! Not only does the 50mm objective lens significantly increase the low light capability during the prime elk hunting times of early morning and evening, but also the field of view is only 63 feet less at 1000 yards.

Alpen Apex # 495, 10X42   Alpen Apex # 499, 12X50

It's important to minimize the amount of pressure that you put on the elk in the course of your scouting. The use of quality optics allows the hunter to cover more territory in less time without having to pressure the game. Also, keep to higher ground when at all possible. Spend more time glassing from prominent lookouts and less time busting brush. Save this for the actual hunt. If you are able to get a fix on these travel routes, it's time to get your map out and plan your ambush taking into account terrain and the prevailing wind.

Finally, give the elk a break on the day before season opens. This is one mistake I see all too often. Hunters with a year's worth of pent up frustration, get to elk camp on Friday before the season opener on Saturday and cannot wait to get out in the woods and find 'em some elk. Do you ever wonder why the elk are all over the place before season and somehow as if by magic they seem to disappear on opening day? Ever think it might have something to do with a few hundred hunters traipsing all over the same hunting area on Friday afternoon between 2:00 pm and dark?

If your plan to bushwhack the elk on the way back from their feeding area fails to produce, then the real tough hunt begins. The elk have made it back into their bedding areas in the timber and if you hope to have a crack at one, you are going to have to go in and get him. In this hunter's opinion, this is the toughest hunting there is, but if you want to hunt where the elk are, during late morning and midday it's the black timber.

Reason # 4...Hunting Short Days and Sleeping Long Nights

Successful elk hunters are committed elk hunters. They are willing to endure hardships that are not typically encountered hunting other North American game. Rising hours before dawn in frigid tents, often without any form of heat, their first act of the day will be to kick off the layer of ice that has formed from the condensation of their breath on top of their sleeping bag over night. **Tip:** Some of the smart ones will have placed their hunting clothing between their sleeping bag and their cot or ground pad, thus helping to further insulate their bedding from the cold and using their body heat to warm the clothing throughout the long fall night. Others are content to just endure jumping into half frozen pants and shirts. Either way, they are up and heading out for elk country with a cup of coffee long before the eastern sky has thought about becoming light. Their daypack is filled with everything that they will require to remain in the field until the last ray of twilight has faded in the west. The thought of coming back to camp for an afternoon siesta has never entered their thinking for these are true hunters. They know that bringing a great bull elk to ground is no simple task. **Tip:** They have planned to stay out every day for as long as it takes. They have waited for these moments all year, and for some...they may have waited for an entire lifetime. These are the men I admire. These are hunters that rarely come home empty-handed.

Reason # 5...Hunting the Easy Ground

Can you hunt elk sitting in a lawn chair on an open hillside five hundred feet from a blacktop road with a cooler full of your favorite refreshment nearby? Absolutely, yes you can. Can you see or even hope to kill elk from such a stand? Maybe. Will you? Hmmmm. My educated guess...more than likely not. While I may have gone a bit overboard with the lawn chair and cooler reference, every year, we see hundreds upon hundreds of hunters who want an easy hunt. They will cruise Forest Service roads sometimes for hours until they spy a particular spot that to them "looks like an elk spot." What does an elk spot look like? How big is it? What color is it? Does it smell like elk? What exactly makes one place look more like elk will appear in it more than another? If someone knows, please tell me!

Anyhow, once they have found their elk spot, they pull the truck and camper out of the center of the road but leaving just enough of the back end sticking out as to cause the next guy coming around the curve a near heart attack. Next this fellow will haul out his trusty rifle, struggle into his one size too small blaze orange vest, and walk a hundred yards down the hill, light up a cigarette and perch himself on a rock for the remainder of the day. This is what some of us call "staking out" the easy ground. Notice that I did not say hunting.

In *Elk Hunting 101* I went to some lengths discussing the fact that elk are herd animals and as such the entire elk population of a given area may pass the sedentary hunter by less than a few hundred yards completely unnoticed. This hunter is far less likely to encounter elk than the hunter who spends his day working hard and wisely covering as much territory as possible.

Reason # 6…Hunting from ATV's

Those of you who have spent any measurable amount of time elk hunting public land knew this one was coming. First let me say for the record, that just like pickup trucks, and campers, and such, ATVs or OHVs or whatever you choose to call them can play a useful role in the overall elk hunting experience. When there are hundreds of pounds of elk on the ground and miles between the hunter and camp, these vehicles when used appropriately and in accordance with the laws and regulations established for the area that is being hunted can be a huge benefit.

Unfortunately each year more and more would-be hunters are taking to the field literally hunting from their ATVs, even though this act is utterly illegal in many states, including my home state of Colorado. If I may by way of a short story, I would like to drive home the extremes to which this abuse has come.

Two years ago I was hunting with a group of friends in south central Colorado. It was mid-morning on the third day of our hunt. I was on a stand overlooking a large meadow in what I considered to be a reasonably remote location a mile or so from the end of the nearest jeep trail and many miles from a designated road. The only trails of any kind in sight were game trails. Hmmm...go figure. How about that? Well anyway, I had been sitting on this particular stand about an hour when I picked up the sound of ....you guess it...ATVs approaching from somewhere down the ridge behind me. Since they sounded like they were coming in my direction I looked at my watch to see how long it took them to get to my position. Almost ten minutes later two guys astride their ATVs came riding down the game trail— in formation— a mere twenty yards behind me, yakking at one another at the tops of their lungs so as to be heard over the cacophony of their machines. I could hear that racket for ten full minutes, and I bet every elk in the area could hear it as well and had for sure left for places unknown far ahead of these fellows. I will not honor what they were doing by calling them hunters. To add insult to injury these two clowns stopped in formation about 50 yards at my 7 o'clock position and decided to take a smoke break with their engines running with me all decked out in blaze orange in clear view. I know this because one of them pointed directly at me. It wasn't until two of my hunting partners walked up the same game trail disgusted by what these guys had just done and joined me, and then the three of us then began to walk in their direction that they came to their senses and hauled buns out of there. What a morning! My hunting partners, Mike and Chad said that they were going to try out another area on the far side of the mountain and I couldn't blame them, so we parted ways and I remained on my stand for a while trying to come up with a new plan.

I thought I had seen it all, but alas I was in for yet another world-class encounter with another real dufus. My huntin' buddies had been gone for about fifteen minutes when I heard what I initially thought was another ATV coming up the trail from the opposite direction, only this one seemed a bit more quiet than the last two. As I continued to look in that direction you can image my shock when low and behold coming up this rocky game trail that is twenty inches wide at best are two clowns in blaze orange hats…. in a front wheel drive blue 2WD minivan! I guess I am a bit slow on the uptake sometimes, but this time I got the point and left to hunt another mountain as well.

For the record, that particular pass that we had been hunting had traditionally held a reasonable amount of elk in seasons past. After this invasion, nobody in our camp saw or heard any elk in that area for the rest of the hunting season. In the years since, we have all discussed that situation more than once and are convinced that the owners of these motor vehicles acting in complete disregard for the hunting and travel regulations of the State of Colorado and the National Forest, literally pushed the elk in that pass into the next county.

If you own an ATV and want to take it with you elk hunting, by all means do so. It is your right. Just remember to respect the right of your fellow hunters and use your vehicle responsibly and within the law.

For what it may be worth, I have been elk hunting the high country for over fifteen years and I have never seen nor met nor heard of anyone who has taken an elk while hunting from any type of motor vehicle. If you need to ride your truck or ATV from camp up a legally marked road to some point of advantage, go for it. Then park it and hunt like the rest of the legitimate hunters.

If you are willing to do the work, hunting dark timber can pay off.
Hunting buddy Danny Farris, Colorado, 2003.

Chapter Five

What Makes For A Great Elk Camp

Hart Wixom in his book *Elk and Elk Hunting* shares with us, "a successful elk hunter can be told by the camp he keeps." In this chapter we hope to give you a few pointers that will help you put together what we believe is a first-class ElkCamp.

Elk hunting is so much more than the actual time spent hiking high country bowls and trudging through deep snows or blow downs in search of Wapiti. Though the average elk hunter typically thinks of "the hunt" as the focal point of his efforts, most agree that it is also a time of fellowship and camaraderie, of nourishment, and rest for our weary souls and worn out bodies. Let's take a look at what can be done to make life in elk camp more hospitable.

Taking a break in our very comfortable two-man camp during second rifle season near Gunnison, Colorado in 2001. The weather was very warm during the day so I never needed the second bag.

The Two-Bag Plan

Every year thousands of elk hunters contact me via ElkCamp.com asking what they should take to elk camp. Most want to know how to prepare for the many possible contingencies that may occur as a result of the finicky weather in the Rockies. If you have ever hunted the high country you know that a typical day of elk hunting may start out far before dawn with frosty single digit temperatures, and by noon the weather can require sunscreen and even shorts, or just as easily you could be overrun with freezing rain or blowing snow. Such is the nature of elk hunting. So how do you prepare for such extremes in the weather?

Since the amount of gear that one can store at elk camp is limited, over the years I have devised what I have come to call my two-bag system. When I start getting my gear out for elk camp I pack two bags, one for the weather that I most expect to encounter, specifically mild weather where temperatures may dip as low as 30 degrees during the day since I usually hunt between mid-September and mid-October, and another smaller bag for my seriously cold weather gear. If you are a late season hunter and expect to spend a lot of time in deep snow and below freezing temps, then forget the smaller bag. All you will need is one large cold weather gear bag.

For those that may be interested, my cold weather bag contains an extra set of well broken-in boots lined with GORE-TEX and insulated with 1000 grams of Thinsulate, an insulated GORE-TEX camo parka, a heavier set of long johns, an extra set of insulated gloves, heavier poly/wool socks, a folding camo flexible stadium seat, and a bucket load of those chemical heat packs. Stadium seat? Yep, these little gems can make all the difference if you're hunting in rain or snow or sitting on a pitched hillside. They save wear and tear on your back and keep your backside dry as well. They are simple seats with a sewn hinge connecting the bottom and back with adjustable nylon straps on either side to control the angle of the back. While these can be found in almost any sporting goods store in a variety of bright colors, mine is a camo version.

A Quality & Roomy Tent Makes All The Difference

For years I hunted from an assortment of small lightweight popup tents mainly because they were relatively inexpensive and didn't take up much room in my vehicle hauling them to elk camp. As I have grown older I have become weary of tripping over bodies in the middle of the night when nature inevitably calls— and I assure you once you pass 40 this is going to happen— stooping and hopping around to get dressed in frosty pre-dawn hours, or having to sleep on a hard, cold ground pad because the tent was not big enough to accommodate a descent cot for my bedroll. Prior to the 2000 elk season, I made one of the best decisions of my hunting career. I purchased a roomy 14x16 foot cotton-canvas outfitter wall tent, and since making that decision, elk camp has never been the same.

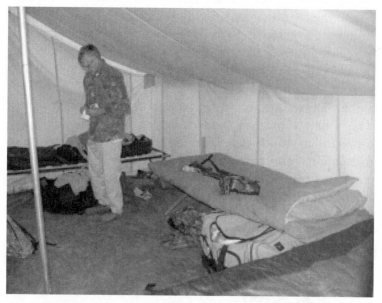

A quality outfitter's tent provides everyone plenty of room. Spencer Ruff shown here in our tent was one my hunting partners during second rifle season in NW Colorado, 2004. As you can see, even with large cots it slept six hunters easily.

Our first outfitter tent slept five hunters very comfortably and we could squeeze another two in if we had to. With five hunters each had more than enough personal space to be comfortable for a week's worth of hunting and then some. Even with a camp stove or propane tank and heater to keep the chill off, there was still plenty of room. The ridgepole running the length of the tent made an excellent support from which a clothesline could be suspended for drying out those wet duds after a long day of hunting. Toss in a few sturdy cots with egg crate foam for mattresses, some old carpet for a floor and you are set.

Recently we upgraded and acquired our newest tent, one that has proven to be one of the best tents we have ever owned from Reliable Tents and Tipis in Billings, Montana. The hexagonal design of our Glacier model creates an openness not found in other tents we have had and the single peak makes the tent more space efficient and easier to heat on fall hunting trips. Since it incorporates a single center pole, one person can easily set up this large tent which can be a real asset if the guy with the tent gets to elk camp early…and alone. The unique and functionally shaped overhanging roof design allows for great wind stability, protects the walls from exposure to wind and water, and provides a very stable foundation to hold up to snow loads. Our Glacier is 17' 8", corner to corner, and 15' 1" wall to wall, each wall is 8' 8" wide. If you are looking for a first-class, sturdy, spacious tent for elk camp, in our opinion Reliable's Glacier is your best bet. See the Glacier at: http://www.reliabletent.com

Reliable Tents and Tipis - Glacier Model Tent
This is our elk camp's main sleeping tent for the 2005 elk season in Colorado.

Why Buy a 100% Cotton Canvas Tent?

In contrast to most of the smaller imported tents that one finds in discount stores, a quality outfitter tent is constructed from heavy-duty 10 to 15-ounce 100% cotton canvas. Unlike tents built from synthetic materials, cotton canvas tents are more durable, insulate better and they can be sealed without having to go to the time, expense and mess of applying seam sealer (see the story about the leaky tent later in this chapter). One of the distinctive attributes of cotton canvas is that when it gets wet, the individual fibers swell and shrink drawing the weave of the material even tighter. This swelling fills in the gaps not only between the individual threads but it also fills the holes left by the needle when the tent was constructed.

To precondition your cotton tent, the tent must be wet down thoroughly. The easiest way to do this is to set the tent up, guying out the sides, the front end and the back end, and stake down the base. If you don't guy the sides, the roof may sag and water may collect above the eaves causing the frame to collapse under the additional weight. Before wetting down the tent, remember to zip or tie the door shut. If the front corners of the tent are guyed out too tightly toward the sides, the zipper door may not operate smoothly. Haul out the garden hose and soak the tent thoroughly making sure to wet all surfaces and seams, and then allow it to dry completely. Check the tent often to make sure it is not straining or sagging. Once the tent is dry, repeat the entire process again. Every time I get a new tent, we go through this procedure. If you wait for a warm sunny day, you can usually complete the process in one day if you start early enough. If you are using a freestanding frame be sure to allow your tent to dry thoroughly on the frame before putting it away. Check the material where it comes into contact with the frame to make sure that it is completely dry. This is usually the last area to dry. <u>Never</u> put a damp tent into storage. If you do, you run a very real risk of the tent mildewing. Mildew is extremely destructive to cotton fabrics and can ruin your tent in short order if allowed to remain on the fabric.

Most tent manufacturers offer a choice of fabrics for your tent. Typically these involve a selection of fabric weights (more weight equals more insulation and a longer fabric life), a flame retardant treatment, and a mildew resistant treatment. All of my tents are ordered with all the above options. The peace of mind is worth the extra cost.

Granted an outfitter tent may require that you spend more cash up front, over the long run however, you will come out far ahead if you take care of your tent. A canvas tent will provide you with many more years of reliable service than most synthetic tents. It will keep you warmer, dryer, and since most are larger than the average discount store model, your accommodations will be far less crowded.

Tip: One last tip on tents, if there is even the most remote chance that you may encounter snow at elk camp, take along a plastic tarp large enough to create a tent fly. Even the most water-resistant materials can leak if snow is allowed to remain on the roof for a prolonged period. This will help to ensure a dry stay at elk camp.

Staying Warm Thru High Country Nights

As you know, while day time temps in the high country during elk season can range from below freezing to well into the seventies during the day, you can bet that when the sun goes down those numbers are going to head south fast, so let's talk about heat in the tent for a moment.

When it comes to managing the temperature inside the tent you have basically three options. One, you can do the Jeremiah Johnson thing and do nothing and just gut it out in what could be a long night in sub-zero temps. Take it from someone who has tried this more than once...when I was much younger. This is not a good idea, not smart, and can quickly take most if not all of the fun out of your hunt. Elk hunting is hard work and requires the hunter to get a good night's rest so that his body can regenerate and get ready for the rigors of the next day's hunt. If you have to spend the night trying to keep from freezing your buns off, how much rest do you think you are going to get?

Ok, there is always one guy who thinks that his gear is good to forty below and he doesn't need any heat in the tent. Here in Colorado, I don't know many places where one can purchase such gear that is probably designed for extended assaults on Everest or K2. If his gear is that good perhaps he wouldn't mind giving up his space in the tent to someone with less technical gear and just sleeping out with the bears.

Option two is to purchase a wood-burning stove and bring in a good supply of well-dried split wood for fuel. There are many quality models to choose from that can be purchased in the $200-$400 range. These are excellent sources of heat and many have optional accessories for heating and retaining hot water for washing up or coffee.

Burning hardwood is better if you have access to it, as it does not produce as much creosote in the flue as softer woods like pine and cedar will produce. Creosote is a black tar like substance that is produced as a byproduct of burning most types of wood. Creosote can build up quickly in the flue and can cause your stove not to vent properly making life in the tent fairly unpleasant if not just plain unbearable. If you find your flue is not venting properly — a good sign is a bunch of smoke in the tent — remove the flue from the stove via the roof hole and try cleaning it out with by tamping it on the ground, or running a long branch down the pipe. If you're burning soft wood like pine for more than eight hours in any twenty-four hour period, be aware that creosote can build up in just a matter of days.

The Wrangler woodstove from Reliable Tents and Tipis.
This stove has a hot water container on the side, which is nice for
washing up at the end of a long day.

Most wood stoves are built tuff, but one thing they are not built to do is feed themselves. In order to generate all that heat throughout long cold high country nights, someone must draw the short straw and assume the duty of getting up around 2:00 a.m. in the morning to feed and stoke the fire. Now don't ask me why you have to do this at such a forsaken hour. There doesn't appear to be any rhyme or reason to how long these stoves will stay hot. I have fired them up as early as 7:00 p.m. and as late as 10:00 p.m. and for some unexplained reason, regardless of when they were lit, they all seem to want to die out around 2:00 a.m. Why 2:00 a.m.? I guess it's because that is when it seems to be the coldest. Go figure? As the guy who has "had the duty," let me tell you, the last thing you want to do when it is freezing in the tent is to crawl out of your sleeping bag thus giving up whatever little warmth you have managed to maintain and walk barefooted across the dirt tent floor or plastic tarp to try your hand at re-lighting a near dead fire in the middle of the night.

I want to share with you a little tale about an eye-opening 2:00 a.m. experience to give you some perspective. The third day of elk season had come and gone and by 8:00 p.m. I was dead tired, so I headed for the bunk tent right after supper. I crawled into my sleeping bag and quickly drifted off. Well, as usual for gentlemen over forty, "the urge" struck around 1:50 in the morning snapping me from my restful bliss and nagging me until I agreed to do something about it. So I hauled myself out of a toasty sleeping bag and took care of business. Upon returning to the tent I crossed over to the woodstove to see if there was any life left in it. Upon opening the door I saw that there wasn't the slightest sign of heat, so being the good guy and thinking of the welfare of my fellow hunters who were still fast asleep, I gathered up some of our special "pre-treated" kindling. An old outfitter had showed us how to keep our kindling stored in an old coffee can about half filled with diesel fuel. Since diesel has a low flash point it burns gradually when lit. Well, as I mentioned earlier, it was day three of our hunt and sometime earlier, I suppose we had run out of our special diesel supply, so some rocket scientist who probably wasn't the brightest bulb in the pack, to this day I don't know who it was, decided he would refill our kindling coffee can with white gas. Can you see where this is going? Sure you can. At 2:00 a.m. in a ten-degree pitch-dark tent, I was unaware of this little change that had been made to our fire starter! So I tossed a few pieces of "special" kindling into the stove and piled about three pieces of split cordwood in on top for good measure. I then struck a common three inch kitchen match and tossed it beneath a piece of the kindling in hopes of bringing some respite from the cold into our cozy little abode. Well as you can guess, the fire lit off all right, just not as I expected. With a whoomp..... that was heard clear across camp, and a flash of striking brilliant orange flame that was probably picked up by the National Reconnaissance Office's satellites in space as some missile launch from Colorado, our little wood stove came to life. For that matter so did every living creature within a few hundred yards of our camp. Fortunately, I was standing just far enough to the side of the opening to avoid becoming the feature attraction of a barbecue. Folks I've seen afterburners on jet fighters that didn't light off that fast! Whew, guess I was living right that day!

In truth wood stoves are the most commonly used source of heat for large tents and have been for decades. When used correctly they can keep the chill off for most of the night.

The third option, and my personal preference by far, for staying warm through the night is a propane-fueled heater. Depending upon the model you choose, these can produce anywhere from 3,000 to 45,000 BTUs of heat. As long as you have propane and you are not somewhere above the Artic Circle, you will stay warm.

The smaller units, like Coleman's Power Cat, run on a single one-pound disposable bottle of propane. I have used one of these to heat smaller 2-5 man pop-up type tents. A single one-pound bottle of propane will keep the heater fired up for approximately eight hours. If you light it off about fifteen minutes before everyone turns in, these smaller tents will be toasty when it's time to hit the sack and it will keep the chill off in all but the most extreme nighttime temps. These can be picked up in most major hunting and fishing stores for around $70.

The next step up is the Mr. Heater® Portable Buddy heater. This unit has two settings (low/high) and can produce up to 9,000 BTUs of heat on a one-pound bottle of propane. Since it is capable of producing more heat it burns fuel at a faster rate and may only last six hours on a single bottle. This unit weighs about ten pounds and can be purchased for around $80.

For those using large wall tents you will need a bit more horsepower to stay warm throughout the night. I use a three-burner type propane heater that mounts to the top of a conventional 20-pound bottle of propane. Each burner can be controlled individually allowing me to produce as little as 6,000 BTUs to as much as 45,000 BTUs. Some may ask, what setting is enough? Let me tell you, if you crank this heater full up to 45K BTUs in a 14x16 wall tent at temps anywhere above zero, it will run you out of the tent in no time.

Here is how I use it. For an average elk season high country night with temps projected to reach down to 15 degrees, I will fire up all three burners on their minimum setting about fifteen minutes before everyone plans to retire. This makes for a very comfortable environment in which to change out of our hunting duds and into whatever we plan on sleeping in. Once everyone is tucked in, I will turn off all but one burner that I leave on a mid level setting (around 9,000 BTUs) for the remainder of the night. This usually is sufficient to keep the tent warm throughout the night. If I wake up and it's a bit chilly, all I have to do is turn up that single burner to get as much as 15,000 BTUs. I have hunted with this setup when the nighttime temps dropped as low as ten degrees below zero and have never had to light off a second burner to keep the tent warm. Using a heater in this manner you can expect to stay comfortable for five to six nights on a single twenty-pound bottle of propane. Since you never know what the weather is going to be like in elk country I always carry a spare twenty-pound bottle of propane just in case a storm blows in and we get stuck in the tent for a few days.

If you elect to use a propane heater inside your tent, there is one warning that you should note. Just like any heater that burns fuel to produce heat, it requires oxygen to keep the burner lit. Where does it get the oxygen? From inside the tent of course. Before you call it a night, make sure that you leave some opening in the tent that will provide adequate replenishment of the supply of oxygen in the tent. Under normal conditions, enough oxygen will make its way into a tent to sustain all those inside, however, these type heaters consume significantly more oxygen. So leave a window cracked or chimney flue flap open to allow an extra amount of oxygen in for the heater. Since a single picture is better than a thousand words, let me share an experience I had a few years ago to emphasize this point.

I had purchased a brand new tent from a major outdoor gear supplier and was anxious to try it out so my hunting partner and I hauled it to elk camp that year. This tent was my next step up from those small pop-ups and I could hardly wait to get it set up and see all the room that it would provide. We arrived at camp on a picture perfect blue-sky 55-degree Thursday prior to the opening of Colorado's first rifle season the following Saturday.

Three of the requirements that I had when purchasing this new tent was that it would be watertight, have plenty of room for up to four hunters, and have a built in floor.

Since it was unseasonably warm for the next few days, I would leave one of the zip-up windows cracked for fresh air during the night. On the third day of the season, as can be the case in Colorado, a storm front moved through and the weather changed dramatically. Blue skies were exchanged for rain and light snow and nighttime temps dropped into the low thirties. After hunting hard for three days, my partner and I had driven into Gunnison, Colorado to treat ourselves to a steak dinner and a bit of civilization that evening. Upon return to camp it was raining cats and dogs so we quickly ducked into the tent, fired up the propane heater and drifted off to sleep with everything zipped up tight to keep out the rain.

About midnight I woke up short of breath and hearing the sound of water hitting the floor. Once the fog of sleep cleared, I looked over at the heater and saw it burning a dull cobalt blue instead of the normal red. Quickly I realized that because the tent was sealed up so tight, the heater was unable to draw air from outside and was consuming much of the oxygen in our tent. I hopped out of my sleeping bag into a puddle of water and unzipped the tent door about twelve inches. Immediately the heater went from blue to its normal red and I began to feel better, all the while my hunting partner was sleeping through the whole event never knowing how close we may have come to tragedy.

Once the more critical issue was taken care of I grabbed my flashlight to see where all the water was coming from. Much to my surprise and disappointment almost every seam in my brand new tent was leaking water from the storm outside. The only dry spot in the tent was directly under the peak of the roof where the pitch was enough to keep the water from coming in. I woke my partner up and we spent the next half hour moving our gear into the only dry area of the tent where we slept until morning. With more wet and stormy weather on the way and a leaky tent, we decided to call the remainder of the hunt off and head home.

Although it has little to do with what heater works best, I'll finish the story. Once I got home, I was to say the least distressed (mild understatement) at the vendor and salesman who had sold me the tent. I had specifically asked the salesman if the tent would require any seam sealer to keep it watertight before I purchased it, and he had indicated that it was ready to go as is and that no such treatment was required. Hah!

After we got home I called the store and asked for the department manager. I told him of the stormy and premature end to our annual elk hunt and that in my opinion it was the fault of his leaky tent. He responded that all tents must be sealed before use to prevent water from coming in through the needle holes. Now I knew that not only was the salesman misinformed but the manager was lacking in knowledge as well, as anyone who has used a cotton wall tent knows, no seam sealer is required as cotton seals itself when it gets wet. Well, back to the story. The department manager and I went round and round for some time until he gave in and said to send it back and they would refund my purchase price. The next day, the faulty tent was on the UPS truck back to the warehouse.

The lesson learned here is to "confirm" what treatment is required to keep your tent dry. What I learned was that while most salesmen are quite knowledgeable about their products, some are not and the consumer has little way of knowing which type of salesperson he is dealing with. Looking back on this event, I now do a thorough amount of research on any product I buy. This way I don't have to rely on the opinion of a salesperson.

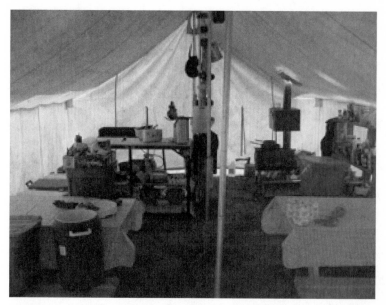

Our outfitter's well-stocked elk camp cooking and dining tent. NW Colorado, 2004

Cooking Gear

Over the years our camp's supply of cooking gear has been amassed from the leftovers from the kitchens of our camp's members. Rather than delve into the details of every item in the camp kitchen, I will hit a few items that I believe can make the difference between a workable camp kitchen and a great camp kitchen.

Our box of flatware looks like a hodgepodge of garage sale rejects. If one could find a single place setting that matches I would be surprised. What does matter however is that we do not use plastic flatware. Granted that disposable plastic is nice and does not require washing, however when it comes to cutting or holding onto a good piece of meat, nothing beats a metal knife and fork.

Coffee is as essential a part of elk camp as a good tent or a well-placed (downwind) latrine. Without it, life just isn't as sweet. Over the years, I have found that there is no substitution for a large stainless steel coffee pot. Ours is a 32-cup percolating version. While 32 cups may seem like a lot of coffee, take it from me; it doesn't take long for three or four guys to go through a pot, especially if they love their morning coffee like I do. If you are like me, you preload the coffee pot with water and coffee the night before so that all you have to do in the cold dark predawn hours is fire up the stove and put the pot on. How many times have you done this only to wake up and find the water in the pot that you left outside frozen solid, thereby turning the coffee preparation process into a half-hour or more nightmare? One way to avoid this problem is to take the preloaded coffee pot into the sleeping tent with you at night. Usually the radiant heat in the tent is enough to keep the water from freezing.

Tip: Here is a coffee-making tip that I learned from an outfitter and good friend of mine, Jim Michaud of Fossil Ridge Guide Service in Parlin, Colorado. A few years ago, I lent my coffee pot and tent to some friends for their camp. When their hunt was over, everything came back as expected except the "innards" for my coffee pot, you know, the percolator stem and coffee grounds cup. For two years that coffee pot sat on the shelf of my garage since I could not find a source to purchase just the missing parts. I was sharing this problem with Jim one day, and he gave me the perfect solution to my dilemma, one so obvious that I kicked myself for not thinking of it on my own. To solve the problem all I had to do was buy commercial coffee in those sealed filter pouches. Toss one or two into a pot of boiling water and wait. After all, a percolator brews coffee by cycling boiling water through the grounds in the upper container. The only missing feature is that you cannot see the color of the coffee through the little view glass on the top of the pot. So when you think it is ready, just pour a bit of coffee into a cup until it looks like you want it to. After a few pots you will know how long it takes to brew to the strength that you like. An added advantage of this solution is that none of the grounds end up in the bottom of the pot for the last cup and all you have to do to clean the pot is to toss the used coffee pack in the trash. Simple, huh?

Another essential for a great elk camp is a large wash pot. There is nothing more frustrating than to try washing up dishes after a meal in some dinky bowl or worse yet, by having no washbowl at all and trying the "pour the soap over the pan" approach. For a few bucks you can find a large canning pot at most surplus stores. These can hold as much as three gallons of water and make easy work of cleaning up. In our camp, we dedicate one burner of our four-burner propane stove for keeping hot wash water going. That way when its time to clean up, you don't have to wait for half an hour for the water to get hot enough to clean the gunk off of your dishes.

Propane Stoves

For years I wrestled with those tiny two-burner white gas stoves for camp cooking. Filling the tank with gas through a tiny funnel (when I remembered to bring it along), then pumping that plunger until my hand and fingers were numb to pressurize the fuel tank. When the propane versions of these came along, I gave up the hassle of white gas and pumping that silly plunger forever. However, it wasn't until I took my first trip into elk country with an outfitter that I learned how the pros do it. They don't fool around playing musical chairs with the small burners on the fold-up stoves; they bring in the heavy equipment, steel propane cook stoves with as many as four high output burners. The heavy-duty steel construction assures years of reliability through even the most frequent use. Many of these come from the factory with built-in collapsible legs that when unfolded and secured place the cook top at a comfortable height for most camp chefs. The burners are placed far enough apart to accommodate large fry pans or pots. Another advantage of these heavy-duty stoves is that the burners can produce as much as 60,000 BTUs of heat for cooking. When hunters start coming back to camp after a long hard day chasing elk, the last thing they want to deal with is a finicky stove that takes forever to heat a pot of hot coffee or grill up some chops. Prices start at around $60 for a basic two-burner version and can run as high as $350 for a deluxe four-burner stove. My three-burner Powder River stove includes an extra large elongated burner designed to evenly heat a huge stainless steel griddle that is included and is great for frying eggs, bacon or cooking up a batch of pancakes. It is made by the Rocky Mountain Range Company of Denver, Colorado and has served our camp and those of many of our friends for almost ten years without fail. A good reliable camp stove is a must for every first class elk camp.

Water Purification

Depending upon where your camp is you may or may not have potable drinking water close at hand. If you can truck in your water great! But if you must use water from a stream or spring for drinking and washing, maintaining a good pure supply is often quite time consuming and frankly hard work if you have to hand pump it through a small water purification system. If you do have to purify your own water, a great solution is Katadyn's Base Camp Micro Filter. This system incorporates a reservoir with a built in filter that can purify 2.6 gallons of water in a matter of minutes. The gravity filter is advertised to remove bacteria, giardia and cryptosporidium to EPA standards, and has an activated-carbon core that keeps water tasting and smelling fresh. It filters up to 200 gallons at a rate of 16 oz. per minute before cartridge replacement. This system is available for around $60.

Another great way to maintain a clean and pure water supply is a Bota Bottle. While this is the trade name for the product I use, there are a number of vendors that make the same thing. As you can see from the photo, this is a simple pull-up-top water bottle with a filter incorporated in the upper part of the bottle. The filter is the same as that found in most water purification systems. All you have to do is open the bottle, remove the filter, fill it from a running water supply, replace the filter, and screw that cap back on. Viola! You have a clean and pure water supply.

J.D.Gossage draws water from a high country stream using his filtered bottle, and then transfers the clean water to his backpack hydration system. Colorado, 2004

If your camp is a bit of a haul from the water supply you might try what my good friend Danny Farris and his partner JD did on a recent backcountry bowhunt here in Colorado. Their spike camp was a bit of a hike from the creek, so rather than run down to the water every time their small bottles ran dry, Danny emptied the contents of his Badlands 4500 backpack and lined it with a contractor grade black plastic trash bag, which he and JD hauled to the creek. As you can see, they then filled the trash bag with a good supply of water from the stream for the next few days and dropped in some iodine tablets for purification. Ah…Necessity, the mother of invention.

Danny Farris and his hunting partner JD Gossage improvising a water transport device on a backcountry bowhunt in Central Colorado, 2004.

The "John"

I realize that for a few this subject may be somewhat of a personal discussion, but for most of us the subject almost borders on the holy. A must for any self respecting elk camp is a well-designed well-stocked latrine, better known in elk country as … "the pooper."

The basics of such include a sturdy seating arrangement (that has nothing to do with straddling a fallen log), privacy, cover (nobody likes going in the rain or snow), a means to keep things sanitary, and a method of keeping plenty of dry paper handy. If you want the deluxe version you can toss in a small propane heater and some hunting magazines though I strongly advise against the last two as they tend to provide far more comfort than is needed thus encouraging folks to spend more time in the pooper than is required, especially if it's really early, really cold, and there is a line of hurtin' hunters waitin' their turn.

If you are looking for a ready-made solution there are a number of retail options available. One of the best I've seen was in our 2004 camp, the Royal Throne produced by Davis Tent and Awning in Denver, Colorado. It is a complete package including a handy 3'6" x 3'6" tent that sets up in minutes, poles, carrying case, and a toilet lid that snaps to a five gallon bucket. This handy package is available for about $135.

If you are more of the do-it-yourself type here are a few tips that will make your stay in elk camp a bit more comfortable. Before leaving for camp there are a few essentials that you will need: 1) An 8x20 foot rip stop tarp with grommets for the walls, 2) an 8x8 foot tarp with grommets for the roof, 3) 50 feet of rope or strong cord, 4) a few used one-pound coffee cans with lids, 5) three to five pounds of commercial lime, 6) a portable toilet seat and stand from a yard sale or health equipment supply house. I found mine at a yard sale for $4. Most of these look like they belong in a retirement home or hospital, but a few cans of camo spray paint will take care of that in short order, and 7) the last item is a small collapsible hand shovel. This will entail a bit of work on your part but once done, this gear will serve you for years to come.

Once you get to elk camp find a location for your privy downwind of camp, preferably in a stand of timber that will allow easy access even in the dark. Often there is one hunter in camp who will use the facility much more than most. This fellow is highly motivated and usually more than willing to volunteer to build the facility. Next locate three small to medium size trees that form a triangle with sides of approximately 6 feet each. If the trunks are not already clear of small limbs up to about 8 feet, you may have to remove a few small branches. Next dig a hole one foot in diameter and about four feet deep (this depends on how many guys are in camp and how long you will stay, a foot per day is a fair rule of thumb) right in the center of the triangle. If you have one, a posthole digger makes this job much easier. Once the hole is complete, wrap the triangle of trees with the larger tarp using the top grommets and rope to attach it to the trees. When you get back to the first tree, simply tie the end of the tarp off at the top thus leaving a nice entryway. Next construct a simple roof with the smaller tarp. Once you have enclosed the privy, use the small shovel to put a small amount of lime into the hole for starters. The lime will help to accelerate the process of breaking down the waste and paper and will also help to control the odor. Now set your handy-dandy seat over the hole, put a roll of paper in each coffee can and snap the lid in place on each coffee can to keep the paper dry and you are ready to rock and roll.

Sleeping Bags

Short changing yourself by arriving at elk camp with an inadequate sleeping bag is one of the quickest ways I know of to wreck what would otherwise be a great hunting trip. When you come to elk camp I strongly advise bringing a quality sleeping bag that is rated to at least zero degrees Fahrenheit. Unless you plan to hunt one of the later seasons in deep snow, a zero-degree bag should keep you warm in most situations. As I mentioned in my previous book, *Elk Hunting 101,* and as most folks who have hunted the high country can attest, weather in the Rockies can and will change on a moment's notice. Early in the 2004 elk season, an unexpected snowstorm that dropped nighttime temps from the low forties to the low twenties hammered many bowhunters in

Colorado. According to eyewitness accounts, one minute the temperature was near seventy degrees with beautiful clear skies, and two hours later the temps had dropped thirty-five degrees and snow was blowing sideways. The lesson here is to be prepared for the worst case that you expect to encounter. You can always crawl out of a bag that is too warm, but take it from one who has been there, you cannot crawl down deep enough into a bag that doesn't have enough insulation. Hunt smart!

Sleeping bags generally come in one of two types, conventional rectangular bags and mummy type bags. If you are large framed guy like me (6'3" and 230 pounds) you will appreciate the roominess of an oversized conventional rectangular bag. Though definitely not designed for backpacking, these bags offer plenty of room in which one can toss and turn in exchange for the extra weight and bulk. For those who prefer lighter-weight or more technical gear, mummy type bags are the way to go. **Tip:** The key to a comfortable night's sleep in a mummy bag is that you must learn that the trick to turning over is to turn the entire bag with you. For years I used to try turning inside my mummy bag before I switched to a conventional bag and the knots I would get myself tied up in would drive me nuts, not to mention keep me awake.

Sleeping bags come filled with a variety of insulations each of which has its advantages and disadvantages. Early designs were filled with duck or goose down and most of the major manufacturers of bags still include down bags in their product line. While few argue that down is an excellent insulator, it does have one major drawback. When it gets damp, the loft collapses and the insulation factor decreases significantly, like to absolutely zero.

Today most quality bags are packed with a synthetic fill such as DuPont Hollofil® 808, Slumberloft HQ™, Polarguard, or

Dupont's Thermolite®. The difference between these is the weight and volume of the fill required to achieve a given level of insulation. My bag is a Slumberjack Big Timber 0°F bag filled with Slumberloft HQ. It weighs in at just over five pounds and will handle most folks up to 6'5" in height.

The best sleeping bag on the planet will not keep you comfortable for a week at elk camp if it rests on hard, cold ground. A good ground pad or cot will make all of the difference. Why not an air mattress you may ask? First, while the air in the mattress will keep you off the ground, the temperature of the air will approximate that of the ground it is resting on. Second, years of observation and experience indicates that most air mattresses tend to lose their air over time. I cannot count the number of times that I have seen hunters awaken to flat or nearly flat air mattresses. If you just must have an air mattress consider one of the self-inflating models. These pads are made of open cell foam encased in an airtight covering. They are popular because they provide the insulation of an open cell foam pad, are reasonably compact when deflated, and offer much of the comfort of an air mattress without having to be blown up. They are however quite a bit heavier than closed cell pads. When you're ready to set up camp, simply open the valve on your sleeping pad and it automatically inflates.

A better bet if you prefer to go light while sleeping near the ground is a combination open cell/closed cell foam pad. These pads feature a thin layer of closed cell (dense) foam that provides a first-rate layer of insulation from the ground combined with a thicker layer of open cell foam for comfort. These types of pads are relatively inexpensive given the amount of additional comfort that they provide. The cost ranges from about $30-$70 depending up the actual features.

For years I have slept on a cot covered with a section of egg crate foam that I got free from a local hospital. The advantage to this arrangement is that I can store all of my hunting gear beneath the cot. This serves two purposes, first the gear serves as additional insulation between the ground and my cot, and second it keeps all of my stuff safe and out of everyone's way. I have one of those cot caddies as well that straps onto the side of the cot with lots of little pockets to hold stuff like glasses, a small book, a roll of toilet paper if needed, and even my rifle if need be.

Finally, don't forget to bring your pillow from home. Sure some guys like to show how manly they are by using a knapsack or some other rolled up piece of gear for a pillow, but honestly nothing will help you to get a great night's rest better than the pillow you sleep with every night. After all, we are talking about creating the ultimate elk camp…right?

Experience Counts…Spread the Knowledge Around

I don't know what your elk camp is like but one of the aspects of our camp that really makes it something to look forward to is everyone is more than willing to share their knowledge and experience with other members of camp, especially if we have younger hunters in camp. As experienced hunters we have an obligation to pass along those lessons that we have learned whether to the less experienced hunters in camp or to those who are new to elk hunting. Years ago, I hunted in a few camps where it was an "every man for himself" atmosphere. To say the least these were not camps that I would consider returning to. Elk hunting is as much about camaraderie as it is about bringing game to ground. Fireside stories and chats and brotherly banter in the cook tent over a cup of coffee or hot chocolate make up a large part of elk camp.

Andy Farris, very respectable 6 x 6 bull, South Central Colorado, 2002

Chapter Six

Understanding and Playing The Numbers Game

Elk hunting is like any other endeavor that encompasses the element of chance. In this chapter I want to help equip you with a more thorough understanding of three important issues that, if factored into your overall elk hunting strategy, will help you to shift the probabilities of success away from the elk and more in your direction. So how do you shift the odds of success into your favor?

Understanding Bull to Cow Ratios

In their ongoing efforts to manage elk herds, one of the objectives of state and federal wildlife managers is to maintain a healthy ratio of bull elk to cow elk in a given area. Typically this ratio is expressed as the number of bulls per hundred cows. For example a ratio of 17:100 indicates that in a given area the herd is estimated to contain seventeen bull elk for every 100 cow elk.

A 6 x 6 herd bull keeping watch over his cows during the 2003 rut.
This is a full-time 24/7 job that leaves the bull tired and worn out going into winter.

Research indicates that higher bull ratios result in improved health for the herd, more hunting opportunity, and increased chances to observe bull elk in their natural habitat.

Bull ratios of 50:100 are optimal for most herds. Following a productive hunting season however these numbers can drop to as low as 7:100 thus placing a strong order on the wildlife managers to do what they can to help get the herd back up to a more stable level. This can be managed by limiting the number of hunters in successive seasons, altering the actual hunt dates to deconflict with more productive hunting seasons during the rut, limiting the types of weapons, modifying the bag limit, limiting the take of bulls to those with four points or more, or reducing the numbers of cow elk in the herd by allowing additional post season hunts to help bring the ratio back in line.

Limiting the number of hunters in a particular area is one of the most effective methods of controlling the number of surviving bulls. When this method is applied to a wide area, this may preclude hunters from hunting every year, which surveys indicate is very important to many hunters.

Second to limiting the number of hunters is managing for age class. This method restricts the harvest of bulls to only those animals meeting or exceeding a minimum age as determined usually by antler growth. In Colorado for example two methods are used to manage for age class. Many Game Management Units or GMUs are limited to the harvest of bulls with four-points or better. This prevents the harvest of most bulls younger than 2 ½ to 3 years of age.

An additional method of managing for age class via controlling the number of hunters is the use of the Preference Point System.

Maximizing and Understanding Preference Points

A number of elk hunting states have incorporated the use of a system of points that a hunter can accumulate over time. This is just one way of managing the number of hunters that can apply to hunt in some of that state's more desirable units, specifically those units that manage the herd for older or even trophy class bulls.

Most preference point systems award a single point to a hunt applicant each year that he applies. Over time the hunter's supply of points continues to grow until his bucket of points reaches the number of points required to be competitive in a drawing for a particular hunt.

For example, here in Colorado, a hunter may select a Preference Point as his number one choice on his annual hunt application and some other limited hunt or an over-the-counter tag as his second, third or fourth choice. In this case the hunter will automatically be awarded a single Preference Point for that year as his #1 choice and possibly some other limited hunt tag as his second choice. This hypothetical hunter is hoping to someday draw a coveted tag to hunt GMU 201, one of Colorado's highly sought-after trophy units that may only award four bull tags per year. In order to successfully draw a tag for this unit a hunter might need to have a minimum of thirteen points in his bucket to be competitive. This means that a hunter would have to put in for a Preference Point each year for thirteen years before he could hope to be drawn. While this may seem like a very long time to wait to be drawn, many including this writer, are more than willing to participate in this process in exchange for a future chance to hunt public land that produces trophy class bull elk.

Waiting out the Preference Point system can at times force a hunter to exercise significant amounts of discipline upon himself. When the goal is ten or more years down the road, a hunter may find himself being tempted to blow his points earlier, say five or six years on a less desirable hunt. This is where the hunter has to really take a hard look at his long-range hunting objectives.

An interim alternative would be to commence a strategy of accumulating Preference points in more than one elk hunting state. This however can become a paperwork and deadline nightmare year after year.

One possible solution to this is to hire a hunting consultant or booking service to manage this application process on your behalf. There are a number of such services around. Each service has a slightly different procedure but in essence the hunter engages the services of the consultant or agent for a nominal fee. Sometimes this fee is paid by the hunter and sometimes it is paid by the outfitter with whom the hunter books. The consultant then assumes the responsibility of determining the hunter's long- and short-term hunting objectives and then accomplishes most of the work required to get the hunter into the system in those states where he hopes to hunt. The consultant will continue to "put in" on the hunter's behalf each year until the hunter is successful in the draw in that particular state. Depending upon the hunting services that one chooses to use, the amount of upfront cash required might vary from a few hundred dollars to the entire cost of each license in the states in which one desires to hunt. The biggest advantage of using a consultant is that these services are provided by a specialist at managing this process and for a fee will relieve the hunter of all responsibility of knowing when and how to put in for elk hunting tags year after year. All the hunter needs to do is write a few checks and then sit back and be patient until the phone rings with those magic words, "you've been drawn!" For a listing of hunting consultants or booking agents, see the appendix in the back of this book.

Statistics and Other Dirty Words

Years ago when I was in college, there were a few words that most of us poverty-stricken students considered so vile as to conjure up visions of demons and the like. These were Algebra, his dreaded brother Calculus, and their evil stepsister Statistics. Someone once said that you could make statistics say anything that you want them to say. I agree whole-heartedly! I am not saying that there is no value to statistics, but just that like anything else, statistics must been taken in context and the source of those statistics should be validated if any measure of credibility is to be assumed.

As they apply to elk herd management and distribution, statistics can be a huge source of information to the hunter doing research on possible places to hunt when viewed in light of the trends as opposed to snapshots at a particular point in time. Most wildlife agencies maintain statistics on elk harvests, success ratios, hunter density, draw potential, etc. on their websites. For the elk hunter who takes the time to study and analyze this information it can give you a real leg up on where the elk are to be found. If you are planning on hunting Colorado, the Colorado Division of Wildlife publishes a Big Game CD (from HuntData). Statistically speaking, this is one of the best tools that I have come across for learning about elk herd characteristics. The deluxe version of the CD can be purchased from the CDOW online for about $100 while the basic version is about $50. Sounds like a lot, but if you are looking for a comprehensive set of stats on elk in Colorado, it's worth every penny.

Not to reflect poorly on those who gather statistics, but more so to suggest that a healthy amount of good judgment needs to be applied to the process, the following story illustrates how the sources of statistics may vary in their accuracy.

About ten years ago, I was planning an elk hunt in southern Colorado where I live. I was vacillating between three areas each of which seemed to have a fair amount of promise. As a part of my homework, I contacted the CDOW officer in charge and made an appointment to drive down and discuss the pros and cons of hunting elk in their respective area.

I called Officer Joe, the name has been changed to protect the innocent, and he invited me to stop by his place the following Saturday. Upon my arrival, Joe came out and suggested that we go inside and have a cup of coffee while we looked over a map of the area. In about an hour I learned more from listening to Officer Joe that I could ever have learned on my own. One of the items of note came about during our discussion of how herd management specialists come up with the estimates on the numbers of elk in a particular herd. Officer Joe's answer was a real eye-opener. According to Joe there were three prevailing methods used for determining the number of elk in a herd. Method one involves the officer flying over the area in an aircraft taking an actual census of elk in the area. The resulting count would be statistically manipulated with a factor to account for the elk that couldn't be seen and a resulting estimate was published. Method two was similar to method one except the census was taken from horseback and on foot. Finally Joe told be about method three. He did offer the disclaimer that this method was not the preferred method, but that he had personal first-hand knowledge of those who had used this method in the past. Method three being the most creative required the officer to predetermine the exact number of animals that would be optimum for his area of responsibility, whip out his calendar and determine a believable time period in which the census would take place, and then proceed to fabricate the entire process with a pencil and calculator from the comfort of his living room table.

Like Joe, I believe that this last method is by far not the rule if it has ever happened at all. It does however, illustrate that the source of statistics can be as valuable a piece of information as the actual numbers themselves. In diplomatic circles, there is a rule that prevails, "Trust But Verify."

As I mentioned earlier, statistics can give a hunter who is doing his homework an excellent picture of trends if one knows what to look for. Rather than look at how many bulls or cows may have been taken in your area last year (snapshot), look at these same numbers say over the past five to seven years. Are the numbers increasing or declining over time? Were there any unusual factors in the observed time period that might have affected or skewed the numbers such as a fire or drought? Did the state allow special hunts in that area that may have changed harvest stats?

Chapter Seven

Camo That Works In Elk Country & Color Vision in Elk

Bowhunters have long acknowledged the inestimable value of wearing effective camouflage when seeking to gain an advantage in pursuit of Wapiti. It has only been in the past ten years or so however, that significant numbers of hunters in the rifle hunting community have come to acknowledge this same truth. For years rifle hunters argued that since their shots would likely occur at long range, there was no need to go to the trouble and expense of buying camo-hunting gear. As many shot opportunities go during rifle season, I might agree with this argument were it not for those times, and we all know of them, when a fine bull or cow has popped up close and silent, catching the hunter "with his britches down" so-to-speak, with little cover in which to conceal his movement while he prepared for the shot. As a result there stands the hunter, a big vertical solid mass that looks and smells in every way to the elk…like a human. The elk's reaction…swap ends and exit the country…now!

On rare occasions I have personally heard a few long-time rifle hunters say something to the effect of, "I don't need no cam-u-flage to kill an elk." Well, I agree, you don't. I have yet to witness or hear of the first elk to be brought to ground by a set of camouflage. I do believe however, that all else being equal those elk hunters who choose to don camo appropriate for the season and surroundings are much more likely to sneak up on and whack a nice branch-antlered bull or a plump cow than those who do not. Let's take a look at a few thoughts and some recent research that supports the argument that good camouflage can make all the difference between success and failure on your next elk hunt.

Color Vision in Elk

Before we go too far down the road on the value of camouflage, here is something to think about that may help persuade you to don a set of camo next time you head out to elk country. At the very least it may cause you to rethink the duds that you hunt in.

Recent research[1] demonstrates convincingly that contrary to much popular opinion of the past, white-tailed deer, and likely by ancestral association their cervid cousin, the elk, possess the anatomical requisites (cones) for color vision and do in fact discern a limited range of colors.

Since this discussion is likely to stir the pot of conventionally held wisdom concerning whether or not deer and elk do in fact discern colors, I want to make it clear that the sources of the research that support this conclusion are from well respected, peer-reviewed individuals and studies in the scientific community and not merely from the personal experience of one or more individuals. For the most part the actual empirical work discussed here was accomplished on deer. However, I personally interviewed no less than three state or federal terrestrial elk biologists plus several state wildlife officials who agree that on a whole, the conclusions contained in this body of research as they apply to deer are very likely to apply to elk as well.

In their study, A Review of Color Vision in White-tailed Deer (Wildlife Society Bulletin, 2003) Kurt C. Vercauteren and Michael J Pipas state that "during the day deer [elk, my emphasis] discriminate colors in the range blue to yellow-green and can also distinguish longer (orange-red) wavelengths. At night deer [elk] see color in the blue to blue-green range." This sensitivity to the blue to blue-green portion of the spectrum peaks in those low light situations as experienced during predawn and late evening or twilight periods. As hunters these are traditionally some of the times that we choose to hunt with greater frequency.

Vercauteren and Pipas further conclude that, "Although deer [elk] can visually detect the color orange, it is the brightness [luminescence] of the fluorescent clothing worn by hunters and not the color *per se* that most likely draws a deer's [elk's] attention. Those who must approach … close [to] deer [elk] without being detected should not wear bright or contrasting clothing, and must respect the deer's [elk's] other senses (hearing, smell) at least equally."

In the course of my interviews, given the regulatory requirement for hunters to wear some amount of fluorescent orange during many elk hunting seasons, it was discussed that this brightness factor of such clothing can be reduced by the wearing of fluorescent orange made from softer materials like cotton or wool, as opposed to those made from harder or more slick vinyl, plastic, or synthetic materials which by their nature are more luminescent or reflective.

Back to Camo

Until recently there were few commercial camo patterns that worked well for elk hunting out here in the West. Most of the readily available patterns were designed to photo realistically mimic eastern hardwoods or marshlands. In my experience these patterns fall short of meeting the need of the elk hunter who hunts low to the ground (rarely in a treestand), above timberline, often in shady dark pine timber, on open rocky talus or sage covered slopes or in juniper brush; or in all of the above.

The purpose of camouflage is to break up the human outline and allow the hunter to become visually indistinguishable from his surroundings. In the course of any hunt we may encounter a variety of environments so we need to ensure that our camo doesn't create a problem rather than solve one. For example, if you are hunting above timberline on a rocky or grass covered slope while wearing a dark forest type camo pattern, you will stand out from the background rather than blending into it. Conversely you will encounter a similar problem while hunting dark timber in a light colored pattern. So what is the solution? Consider two sets of camo. I typically carry one of each to elk camp, a dark set for black timber and a very generic lighter set for hunting open ground, because I do not know from day to day what type of ground I will be hunting. Some of you are bound to ask; do I come back to camp and change during the day or carry the other set in my daypack? Well I have been accused of being a bit on the anal retentive side, but I'm not that anal. In most cases I do not go to this extreme unless I find myself back in camp for other reasons.

When its time to purchase that next set of camo, consider the type of terrain and cover that is predominant in the areas that you hunt. If you hunt higher elevations where the elk are often found during pre-rut and the rut, you may find that you are hunting above timberline a lot and need a pattern that works well in the open and on rocky slopes. In this environment patterns that resemble hardwoods, or marshes could even work against you. What you will need is an open pattern of generic shapes that includes a mixture of muted shades of gray and green to help you blend in more with sage, cactus, and rocks.

Late morning and midday when the elk have moved out of their feeding areas and back into the black timber to bed down can be, in my opinion, some of the most productive times to hunt. Rather than being on the move from one area to another, elk are more sedentary during these midday hours as they rest and digest. When hunting densely forested areas and blow downs, you will want to consider using a darker more 3-D camo pattern that blends in well in a pine type environment that is dominated by shadows and deadfalls.

Marc Carlton shows us how well a good camo pattern can work in the right environment.
Vanish Camouflage by CamoWest

"Vanish", a newly released pattern (shown above) created by friend, veteran elk hunter, and calling legend Wayne Carlton is an outstanding camo for the elk hunter who spends more time hunting dark timber and fringe areas where elk hold up during the middle of the day. CamoWest's Vanish exhibits an unsurpassed depth of field not found in other camo patterns. CamoWest's extreme attention to three-dimensional detail in Vanish is what makes this incredible pattern stand out from its competitors. If you really want to disappear in dark timber, check out Vanish at CamoWest.com. and major sporting goods suppliers.

What Triggers the Flight Response in Elk?

Have you ever thought for sure that you were busted when a bull or cow looked you dead in the eye from close range? Yet for some unexplained reason they continued to feed or go about their business. For one I have seen this behavior dozens of times in the field and on film as well. A friend of mine recently produced a nice video on elk that depicts various scenes of large bull elk. In more than one case, the bull will curiously look directly at the cameraman, but lacking any clue as to what the object of his attention is, he continues to graze only occasionally glancing back in the direction of the camera. Let's look at why elk exhibit this type of behavior.

My theory and that of many of the elk biologists and professionals in the field that I interviewed in the course of doing research for this book explains this unexpected behavior. It is what I like to call my "Two Strikes and You Are Out Theory."

The self-protection mechanism of elk depends primarily upon external input to their three primary senses: smell, sound, and vision. Because an elk's sense of smell has been so finely attuned to detect danger over thousands of generations, in the case of a snoot full of "man odor" elk may elect to trigger or flee with just this one sense receiving input. However in situations where elk receive input from either their hearing or vision, I believe and many situations such as the one discussed above support this theory, that while elk may alert (show interest) with only one sensory input, they will likely not trigger (flee) until that initial sensory input is confirmed by input from a second self-defense sensory system, i.e. two strikes and you are out.

The Bull and the Bowhunter

To help make my point, try to visualize this scene that I saw about a year ago while I was watching a video produced by the manufacturer of a scent cover-up product. In this particular scene a rather nervous bowhunter is seen kneeling behind a fallen log covered from head to toe in camo and presumably a host of scent containment systems. His trusty bow is right there in his hand but alas the hunter is as fixed as a marble statue incapable of movement. Why? Well almost certainly because this monster bull elk is standing over the hapless hunter at what appears to be less than two feet with his nose about six inches from the poor bowhunter's left ear. Strike one.

This business of the bull elk trying to determine who or what this funny looking critter behind the log is continues for what seems like minutes. To his credit — and possibly his longevity — the hunter remains completely motionless throughout most of this encounter. Surely his thoughts during this "time of trial" are less on whether or not he will be successful in his hunting efforts, but likely more so on whether or not he will make it through the event with clean shorts or even if he will survive the day. After what seems to the viewer like a very prolonged engagement between the bull and the bowhunter, it appears that the hunter could no longer stand the strain and moves just a hair. Strike two! The bull immediately detects this ever-so-slight movement and does a one-eighty and hightails it for parts unknown.

Clearly in this situation the bull could see the hunter, otherwise why would he have continued to indulge his interest for so long? But without additional clues from his other senses, i.e. motion, sound or scent, the hunter remained…merely a curiosity. Once the bull's vision sense picked up a second clue…movement, the bull's self-preservation mechanism kicked into gear. Putting one and one together made for strike two. The bull recognized the hunter for what he was, a potential threat, and the bull triggered or reacted accordingly.

As I mentioned at the beginning of this chapter, camouflage remained for years an integral asset of the bowhunter. Today more and more bowhunters are choosing to put their entire camp on their back and head out for the backcountry leaving eighty percent or more of their fellow hunters behind is search of those elusive big bulls. Our next chapter is courtesy of my best friend and hunting partner, Roger Medley. This brief excerpt from Roger's forthcoming book, *Backcountry Bowhunting* will give you a brief glimpse into some of the many advantages of this type of hunt as well as some of the challenges that one can expect.

Backcountry bowhunting means taking your camp with you on your back as you follow the elk. It means making the shot regardless of the angle.

Chapter Eight

Backcountry Bowhunting
with Roger Medley

Soon after moving to Colorado in September of 2000, my wife and I headed out to do some last minute scouting for the upcoming elk season in an area southwest of Gunnison in south-central Colorado. The valley in which we decided to setup camp was spectacular, stretching about four miles to the north and another couple of miles to the south. The north-facing hillsides were covered in heavy, dark timber and a small picturesque brook flowed down the center of the valley floor. The fall air was crisp and clean, invigorating us as only the high country can. We had arrived late in the day so we immediately began the process of setting up camp and rehydrating our dinner of backpacker's dehydrated lasagna. Our bellies filled to the brim we crawled our dog-tired bodies into our sleeping bags for a much-anticipated night's sleep. When our heavy-eyed heads finally hit the pillows it was 10:00 pm.

We could not have been down for more than five minutes when my wife and I were startled by a piercing racket coming from the north end of camp. In as brave a voice as she could muster my wife asked, "wha…wha…what's that?" As I started to lie back down, I turned to my wife, grinned and said, "Shasta, that's why we're here. That's a bull elk bugling!" That elongated lonesome bawl of the first bull acted as a catalyst setting nearly a dozen other bulls into motion. Before long the elk were serenading us and every other living creature in the valley. For nearly two hours we were surrounded by elk song before things began to settle down and we finally drifted off to sleep with dreams of bugling bulls dancing about in our heads.

Sometime later during the night, my wife, not being accustomed to sleeping in such proximity to large horned critters with only a small nylon tent to protect her, was again awakened and asked, "Did you hear that?" Dead to the world, I told her not to worry and go back to sleep. I'm not sure how much sleep she got. The next morning we decided to check for tracks and to our surprise discovered that an entire herd of elk had passed right through our camp during the night! Their tracks told the story. They had walked right around our little tent. What my wife had heard during the night was the sound of the elk crushing the frozen snow right outside our tent. We were at least six miles from any paved road – we were where the big boys roam.

As a rule few elk hunters venture more than three or four miles from where they camp or park their vehicle. I've been in elk camps where a hunter returned to camp well after dark boasting to his fellow hunters of having discovered where the herd was holed up, only to deliver the bad news that they were about four miles from camp. Wouldn't it be nice if getting to the elk in the morning didn't require getting up at 2:00 a.m. or earlier and hiking four miles over unknown ground in the dark? Knowing that the average hunter can cover about one to two miles per hour, depending on the terrain, you may ask, is there another alternative? You bet! Have you ever tried backcountry bowhunting?

What is Backcountry Bowhunting?

What do we mean by backcountry bowhunting? I'm sure that you've heard the term or read it in one bowhunting magazine or another. Simply put, backcountry bowhunting means taking the hunt to the elk. It entails continuing one's hunt beyond the point where most other elk hunters call it a day and begin the trek back to camp well ahead of official sunset thus leaving the elk and wasting what many agree are the best hunting hours of the day. It means carrying your entire camp along with you on your back, hunting and camping right out of your backpack. Should you strike a fresh track or come across a herd late in the day yet too far to make a successful stalk without getting busted, you have the ability to back off, set up camp, and be back on the elk first thing in the morning. Chances are that they will be right where you left them the evening before or very close by.

By remaining within reasonable proximity to the herd that you've chased all day you won't spend all that time and energy hiking back to camp just to have to get up extra early the next morning and do it all over again to get back on the elk that you left a few hours ago. Whether you choose to go all out and hunt the entire season this way, or you just want to spend a night or two away from your base camp, there are a few things you'll want to consider specifically regarding gear.

Backcountry Gear…Think Light and Multi-Purpose

When it comes to backcountry gear, think lightweight and multi-purpose. The bandana is a great example. A bandana is an inexpensive and lightweight solution for a number of backcountry needs. If you make it out of a camo material, you can use it as a dew rag or a facemask. It can also double as a handkerchief or a first aid sling in the event of injury, or even a camp washrag. Remember…think multi-purpose.

When you are miles from a fresh water source, how will you provide for your water purification needs? Will you boil the water? If so, you'll need more fuel for your stove – that's extra weight. How about using one of the many water filter purification systems? Whether you use a filtered pump type system, a gravity system, or a filtered bottle, all of these incorporate filters that will eliminate most of the harmful organisms commonly found in streams and lakes such as Giardia or Cryptosporidium.

A bivy camp allows the hunter the utmost in flexibility.
He can stay put or move with the elk as necessary.

What about shelter? Tent manufacturers are making great strides in the single-wall tent market. A single-wall tent can save you many pounds of weight! It does however come with a fairly hefty price tag. A less expensive and lighter solution that I've opted for is a bivy sack and a silicon impregnated tarp. A bivy sack is basically a waterproof bag that your sleeping bag fits into. My entire shelter system weighs about two pounds. When the alarm clock goes off, I leave my down sleeping bag in my bivy sack, roll it up and I'm on my way in the morning in record time compared to taking down a tent and sleeping bag separately. Leaving my bag in my bivy sack protects it from rain and snow should I encounter any. The weight saved by using a bivy sack in lieu of a tent can add up to several pounds. Affordable lightweight backpacking tents weigh in around three to four pounds. Bivy sacks tip the scales at a mere one to two pounds. By using a Bivy sack you also add about ten degrees to the effectiveness of your sleeping bag, allowing one to use a bag rated for a warmer temperature, thus saving even more weight.

If the weather is looking questionable for your backcountry hunt,
a lightweight tent may be called for.

Should you choose to go the tent route, there are some definite pluses. Most tents will provide you with enough extra room to store your gear inside your tent or the vestibule. If you're waiting out a storm that lasts most of the day, having dry gear close at hand is a real plus. While the tent will add more overall weight to your backcountry rig, the trade-off may be worth it. The decision is yours.

Campsite Location Considerations

When selecting a site to set up a backcountry camp for the night, it is a good idea to avoid valley floors especially near streams. Weather 101 tells us that cold air being heavier than warm air will sink and the coldest air will seek out the lowest point in the valley. Find a location about fifty feet above the valley floor and you'll stay much warmer. In fact, I've seen a temperature difference of fifteen degrees warmer just fifty feet above the valley floor. Plus you won't run the risk of the stream overflowing from a downpour during the night and flooding your campsite. Since you will be sleeping in a warmer environment, this practice may allow you to save some weight by bringing a lighter weight sleeping bag.

Can You Make the Shot?

While, these are just a few things to consider when getting ready for backcountry bowhunting, what it really comes down to is making the shot. A couple of rather critical issues the backcountry bowhunter should ponder include: canting your bow and up/downhill aiming when your target does not present you will a shot on level ground.

Shooting target archery has opened my eyes to the use of a level on all my sights. A level will prevent me from canting (tilting) my bow to the left or the right. Some wonder just how much difference a level makes. Let me give you an example of just how important having a level on your sight, and using it, can be.

While preparing for a tournament not too long ago, I noticed that my arrows were impacting consistently to the right about three inches. I'd made no change to any of my equipment, so where was this problem coming from? I put my bow on a device used to see if the level in my sight was actually square with my bow. I found that the sight had come loose and was off by only half a bubble, which was causing me to cant my bow very slightly to the right. I guess one could say that for a time, I was about half a bubble off of plumb. Half of a bubble is almost indiscernible while at full draw. Consider this, a three-inch error at twenty yards equates to six inches at forty yards. An error of six inches can mean a miss, or worse, a non-fatal wound. In my opinion, the use of a level on your sight is essential.

Now that you've ensured that you won't inadvertently cant your bow, how do you compensate when shooting up or downhill? You've ranged the bull at 28 yards downhill from you, but what distance do you aim for? Do you aim above the bull or below? Up and downhill shots can be real stress producers for those who haven't made many of these shots. Let me put you at ease, understanding what to do is really pretty simple. When aiming up or downhill there are two factors to consider, the horizontal distance to the target and the angle to the target.

The horizontal distance to the target is the distance from the archer to the target as if they were on the same plane or level. In the example below, the horizontal distance is 20 yards, while the straight-line distance is actually 28 yards. The way I judge the horizontal distance is I pick a tree near the target and draw an imaginary line straight to a point at eye level. This is the distance I judge or range. In the example this distance is twenty yards.

The second thing to consider is the angle at which you're shooting. In our example, the angle is 40 degrees.

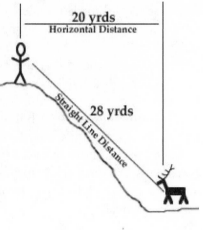

For greater computing detail see the chart below. Follow the 20-yard line row to the right until it intersects the vertical 40-degree column. They intersect at 15.3 yards. According to the chart you'll want to **aim** (pin selection) **as if the shot is 15.3 yards.**

The Hip-Pocket Solution: Estimate the horizontal distance and aim using a distance slightly less. How much less? It depends. The steeper the angle, the more you will subtract from the horizontal distance.

	Angle From Level (up or down)			
	10°	**20°**	**30°**	**40°**
Horizontal Distance (Yds.) NOT straight line distance)				
10 YARDS	9.8	9.4	8.7	7.7
20 YARDS	19.7	18.8	17.3	15.3
30 YARDS	29.5	28.2	26.0	23.0
40 YARDS	39.4	37.6	34.6	30.6
50 YARDS	49.2	47.0	43.3	38.3

Roger Medley's book, *BackCountry Bowhunting* previewed here, will be available from Jackson Creek Publishers Summer, 2006. Look for it at ElkCamp.com and at bookstores everywhere.

Roger Medley, www.backcountrybowhunting.com

Jay's Thoughts On Picking the Perfect Backcountry Bow

I have been bowhunting since age fourteen, starting out with a lightweight Ben Pearson recurve then graduating to stronger and shorter recurves like the venerable Super Kodiak and Kodiak Magnum. In the early 90s I made the jump to a compound bow by purchasing a well-used PSE Polaris. The Polaris had a host of features that I didn't like the least of which were it had a low let-off, and it was really short for a bow of that time. I was still a finger shooter in those days and the acute angle of the string and my thick fingers never got along all that well, so the Polaris spent most of its life hanging in my garage until I gave it to a hunting buddy. Since that time almost fifteen years ago, I have owned a variety of compound bows of all shapes and manufacture. For years I had been a strong advocate of longer axle-to-axle bows with high brace heights knowing that such a combination would provide for more consistency and forgiveness in my shooting, both of which I could use in large quantities. The trend however in compound bows since about 2003 has been towards shorter and shorter bows, which I avoided like the plague because of my earlier experience with short bows.

In 2001, my doc told me that I had to have shoulder surgery to repair damage to my right shoulder. That put a damper on my bowhunting for about a year. Then the doc told me that I would need a similar procedure done on my left shoulder. Yep, another year of bowhunting down the tubes. 2003 was taken up with writing *Elk Hunting 101*, and 2004 ended up with me being tossed by the horse that you read about in chapter one. So, for a total of almost four years, my bowhunting career was almost zero. All healed and ready for the 2005 elk archery season I took inventory of my gear and came to the conclusion that my now almost six-year-old bow had seen its day. Thus I began my research for what I believed would be the best bow for me.

Believing that all decisions should be informed decisions; I spent weeks and weeks pouring over bowhunting magazines and websites. I talked with archery shop owners and the shooters that frequent them. I even asked questions on every bowhunting online forum I could find seeking to learn as much as possible. Surprisingly, I discovered that not only are most shooters quite passionate about the bows that they shoot, they are also emphatic that each of them is right! So what did I do? I starting shooting bow after bow looking for the bow that best suited me. I knew that I wanted a bow that featured parallel limb technology to help reduce the amount of noise and hand shock. I also wanted a single-cam bow. It is my opinion that while all compound bows have timing issues, those with two cams tend to have more than single-cam bows. While many two-cam shooters argued that their rig was the best, none argued with my premise that single-cam bows have fewer timing issues than two-cam bows.

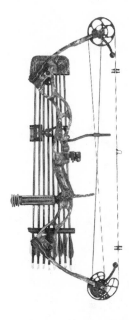

After months of research, I finally made my decision, a brand new PSE Vengeance NRG One-Cam. At only 33 ½ inches axle-to-axle, my 2005 PSE Vengeance is deadly accurate. To emphasize how finely tuned PSE has made this bow, on my first test shot with the Vengeance at twenty yards, arrow #1 hit 2 inches at 7 o'clock. When I released arrow # 2, I heard a crack and saw something fly across the room downrange. Thinking I had broken the store's bow, I timidly asked the pro shop manager what happened? He just smiled at me and said, "Jay you just shot the knock off the first arrow." The pluses didn't stop with accuracy, as I continued to shoot I noticed how quiet the bow was and that handshsock was virtually absent, all major selection criteria for me. Weighing in at just 4.1 lbs. and boasting a very quick IBO speed of 303 fps, it is like firing lightning bolts compared to its predecessors. For backcountry bowhunting PSE's Vengeance is the bow for this serious bowhunter.

Ultimately, choosing the perfect backcountry bow for you is not a matter of someone else's opinion. It should be your opinion. You can and should do all the homework possible before making this decision, but make sure that before you make your final decision, you head down to the range and shoot every bow that you are considering. It all comes down to what bow shoots best for you.

Chapter Nine

So You Think You Need A Horse

Every year I get thousands of calls, emails, or contacts of some kind from hunters wanting to come out West for an elk hunting adventure. Many of those ask my opinion about the use of horses for their hunt. Most have watched hunting videos or cable TV showing elk hunters astride these beasts traveling through extensive picturesque valleys and over monstrous mountains in search of Wapiti. Bearing in mind the great distances and breathtaking vertical challenges that accompany elk hunting, they see the use of a good horse or mule as not only a part of the western experience, but a solution or possibly salvation from the rigors of having to accomplish the hunt on foot. That being said, briefly my thoughts on the use of horses or mules are these.

Advantages… or the work they save you

There is no question that horses or mules, your preference if you know the significant differences, can make getting you and your gear back into some great elk country a much easier task. A good packhorse with saddle panniers can pack in or out as much as two hundred pounds (120-150 pounds is average) of gear depending upon the size of the horse. Horses allow you the freedom to travel far from roads and other hunters. Clearly a horse will provide the hunter with a source of ready reliable transportation that will allow him to cover far more territory during a day's hunt than the hunter ever would have been able to cover on foot. Should you get an elk on the ground, a well-trained horse or mule that is acclimated to the smell of blood and has no problem hauling something on its back that was recently a living, breathing creature is worth its weight in gold. All you have to do is haul an elk a few miles out of the backcountry on your back, one quarter at a time to appreciate what I am saying. All these advantages being quite clear let's look at the other side of the equation.

Disadvantages…or the work they cause you

Horses like hunters require a certain amount of attention and care each and every day. Like us, they must rest, eat and drink regularly, even more so because they are doing most of the work of hauling your buns around the mountains all day long. This means that in addition to your own food, you will need to pack feed for your horses into camp. You may think that you can just allow the horses to graze in a nearby meadow for their nourishment. To some extent this does work depending upon what is growing in the meadow and whether or not there is a lot of deep snow on the ground that would prevent the horses from getting to the grass below. If you are really working the horses hard or if the temps start to get low at night, you will want to supplement their diet with grain, which has to be purchased and packed in as well.

Next you will need to have a plan for how you plan to keep the horses close to camp at night. Will you hobble them? Will you put them on a line? Or will you pack in a portable battery powered fence?

What will you do if one or all of your horses gets loose and runs off? If it is your horse, I assure you, your hunt will cease and you will do whatever it takes to locate the animal. If it is not your horse as in the case of a rental, I assure you, your hunt will cease and you will do whatever it takes to locate the animal. Bottom line, if a horse gets loose and wanders off, everything stops until the horse is located and returned to camp. This may take only an hour or so, or…it may take days. Either way, your hunt is on hold until the horse is located.

What will you do if a horse becomes sick or injured? Do you have the knowledge or skills required to take care of the animal? If so, great! If not, you have got a major problem on your hands.

Preparing your horse for a day's hunt will require whoever is responsible for the animal to get up as much as an hour earlier than you plan to leave camp to water, feed, and saddle the horse. At the end of the day, everything is in reverse regardless of how late you may get back to camp. If it has been a long hunt and you do not get back to camp until 9 or 10 p.m. at night, you are dead tired, hungry, and ready to hit the sack, but guess what, you still have to feed, water, unsaddle and care for your horse.

These are just some of the challenges a hunter will need to consider if he is thinking of taking a horse or mule along on his hunt. If the horse is your own, then you will already know all of this and you will come prepared. If the horse is a loaner or a rental and you are not thoroughly knowledgeable and experienced in the care and use of these wonderful animals, I suggest you exercise one of three options: 1) Hire a professional outfitter to take you on a fully guided hunt. 2) Hire a professional horse wrangler who will assume all responsibility for the animals to accompany you on your hunt, or 3) forget the idea of using a horse and get ready to hunt on foot.

"Conway", a dependable mount who just didn't like porcupines.
NW Colorado, 2004

Chapter Ten

A Good Hunting Consultant Can Save You Money & Aggravation

I have been a professional hunting consultant for almost ten years. I became a hunting consultant to help other hunters avoid some of the less obvious pitfalls that one can encounter when you are looking into a hunt and have little experience in where to go, or who to trust. Our first-class reputation is why thousands of elk hunters contact us each year and over six million of you visit us at ElkCamp.com annually seeking information on this great adventure we call elk hunting. Why should you engage the services of a reputable hunting consultant? Since a picture is worth a thousand words, let me share with you the following account of a very good personal friend, Tracy Breene, who was duped by an unprincipled individual who called himself an outfitter. This is a brief excerpt from Tracy's story as shared by Tracy himself in my first book, *Elk Hunting 101, A Pocketbook Guide to Elk Hunting*. With Tracy's permission, I share it with you again in hopes that you will see the value of allowing a consultant to help you sort out the wheat for the chaff.

> Often times when Easterners head out West, our heads are dancing with dreams of what we think elk hunting really is. We may have a good idea of what elk are and what hunting them is like, but something that is foreign to many of us is that we don't always know what to expect from an outfitter. This is especially true if you have never had the privilege of hunting with a guide.
>
> Although I am an experienced hunter, finding a good outfitter can be hard and often times there are just as many bad outfitters as good. On a recent [2003] trip to Colorado, I searched for weeks before I made the final decision on an outfitter to hunt with. Why did I choose this guide? He said all the right things. He knew what to tell me to convince me that his was a first-class and reputable outfit, but he was crafty enough not to tell me too much. I was told we would have Class-A accommodations. I was told I would be into elk every day. I was told I would be hunting with experienced guides. I was told I would have a 90% chance of getting a shot. I ate this up like a kid in a candy store. Unfortunately, Class-A accommodations turned out to be a pop-up camper with a propane heater, and we never saw an elk. Needless to say, we never got a shot and from my point of view our guides didn't have any experience guiding bowhunters.
>
> Another method is to use a hunting consultant like Jay Houston of ElkCamp.com. A good consultant

carefully researches the outfitters he uses and has learned over time what hard questions to ask of a new outfitter. Elk hunting is just that - hunting, and even if you do not see elk, you want to have a good time. Any well run operation will try their hardest to put you on elk, and if that is not possible, they will at least show you a good time and give you lasting memories. Just remember one thing when talking to outfitters that is also true in life: If it sounds too good to be true, it usually is. If your gut feeling tells you a certain outfitter is trying to pull the wool over your eyes, cross him off the list!!!   God Bless, Tracy Breen

As an update to Tracy's story, Tracy had the opportunity to return to Colorado for another bowhunt in 2004, and bagged his first bull elk while hunting at the famous Three Forks Ranch. I spoke with ranch manager, Jay Linderman, some months after Tracy's hunt. Knowing full well the unfortunate experience that Tracy had endured in 2003, Jay told me that his team was determined to do their best to help Tracy achieve his lifetime goal of harvesting a nice bull. On the fifth day of his hunt Tracy's dream came true when he harvested a very nice 5 x 5 bull. Good job Tracy!

Hunting consultants are not the solution for everyone. But if you don't live in or near elk country and don't know where to start planning your hunt or who to trust, consider contacting a reputable hunting consultant. It is our job to help hunters locate exactly the right hunt, while avoiding problems like the one Tracy encountered. I work full time throughout the year identifying quality hunts, ranches, and outfitters that I can refer my hunter clients to. When I am not hunting, writing, or filming, I am traveling to visit with our team of outfitters and ranch owners looking for the best opportunities for those who choose to place their trust in our services.

Chapter Eleven

Field Dressing Your Elk

Now the real fun—spelled w.o.r.k. — begins. Ok so you have somewhere between five hundred and a thousand pounds of elk lying on the ground at your feet. What do you do?

While it is not impossible to dress out your elk alone, the task will be much easier if you have a hunting partner to help. A partner comes in handy for help in stabilizing the animal and when it comes time to pack the rascal back to camp.

1. The first thing you will want to do is to position the animal with the head uphill and the tail downhill. This will help facilitate draining blood and fluids from the body cavity once you open the critter up.

2. With a sharp knife, make a deep cut completely around the rectum making sure not to puncture or cut the intestine. Pull the end of the rectum to make sure that it is separated from the tissues connecting it to the pelvic canal. Take a piece of string or a strong rubber band and tie off the end of the rectum to prevent droppings from escaping and touching the meat.

3. Roll the animal onto its back. This can be a challenge if you are alone or if the animal is on a slope. If the animal is on a slope and there is no way you can move it to level ground, then look for a nearby tree or bush on the uphill side of the animal. Take a length of rope and tie it off on the uphill front leg then tie the other end to the tree or bush tightening the line to keep the animal on its back or as close as you can get. If you have a partner, have him steady the animal on its back while you straddle the critter facing to the animals rear. If you put your right leg right behind the elk's leg to your right and your left leg in front of the elk's leg to your left, this will further help to stabilize the elk as you begin to work. If you are working alone, this same 'sit astride' technique works about as well as any.

4. Make a shallow cut through the skin just below the breastbone. If you plan to cape the animal you will want to ask your taxidermist how he prefers you to cut the cape and remove the hide. At the point of the initial cut insert the index and center fingers of your other hand through the cut facing the elk's back end. Carefully insert the knife with the blade facing away from the body between these two fingers. The fingers form a guide for the blade as you begin to work it through the hide all the way to the back of the elk. Note: if you are dressing out a bull, you may want to remove the genitals prior to making this cut. Bull elk often urinate on themselves and by removing this part you minimize the possibility of contaminating the meat with urine. To do this, just prior to the penis and sheath, direct your cut around the

genitals to the left and to the right coming together again near the cut you originally made to free the rectum. Now skin the entire penis and sheath from the animal all the way back to the testicles. Cut the muscles and tendons pulling everything to the rear of the animal. Some states require that evidence of sex remain attached. If this is the case in the state in which you are hunting, be sure to leave either one testicle (bull) or some portion of the mammary gland (cow) attached to the abdominal wall. If your state does not require this, you can continue to remove the genitals all the way to the rear. Some minor cutting and tissue remove will be required to accomplish this. Make sure that the hide is cut all the way to the pelvic bone.

5. Now that you have cut the hide and separated the genitals, you can go back to where you made the cut in the chest and make a second cut along the same path through the abdominal wall all the way to the rear. Be very careful that while making this cut that you do not cut too deep and puncture the paunch (gut). If you err and cut too deep you will know it almost immediately that you messed up as you will be rewarded with a unique and almost overwhelming stench that you never knew existed as gut gasses begin to escape. Once this cut is complete all the way back to the pelvic bone, you can reach into the area below the pelvic bone and extract the tied off rectum pulling it back into the cavity.

6. To remove the viscera (guts) you will need to reach as far forward inside the body cavity as possible and cut the windpipe and esophagus. This can be a bit messy, but it has to be done, so just get on with it.

7. Once you have cut the windpipe, the entire gut can be removed by using both hands to pull it away from the inside of the body cavity. You may have to make one or two small

cuts if something hangs up, but the internal organs should all come out at once with little effort.

8. Continue to drain as much blood from the cavity as possible.

9. The next step is to begin removing the hide. While there are a few advantages to leaving a hide on if you have to drag the carcass some distance, the disadvantages far outweigh any advantage of leaving the hide on. As soon as the animal dies bacteria will begin to form in the meat. By removing the hide you allow the meat to cool faster thus slowing the process of bacterial growth. By cooling the meat immediately you are doing the best you can to preserve the quality of the meat. Unless you manage to kill your elk in camp or while it's standing in the bed of your pickup, you will want to quarter the animal for transport anyhow.

10. When skinning an elk, a good place to start is just above the center joint in the leg. Inserting your knife at this point just inside the leg, you want to make a cut all the way to the chest. Then return to the point where you started the cut and cut completely around the leg cutting from inside the hide to outside. By cutting from inside to outside you avoid getting hair on your meat and your knife will stay sharp much longer since it isn't having to cut through hair. Repeat this process for all four legs.

11. Once all four legs have been skinned you can begin the process of skinning the hide away from the body itself. I prefer to work my way from the original chest cavity cut up towards the backbone, working on one side at a time. Once the entire hide on one side has been cut away, lay the hide, hair side down, on the ground away from the body making sure not to get dirt on the exposed inner side of the hide. When the entire hide from one side has been skinned back to the backbone, you can begin the quartering process.

12. Quartering an elk is made easier with the use of a bone saw. There are any number of these made specifically for hunters available at your local sporting goods retailer. After skinning one side of your elk, with it lying on its unskinned side, you will want to remove the head and all four legs. The head can be removed using your knife and saw just behind the ears. This leaves the maximum amount of neck meat remaining. With your saw, cut the legs off just below the joint where you began the skinning process. Next separate the front quarter from the rear quarter by making a cut behind the rib cage. As hindquarters are heavier than front quarters, you will want to think about how far forward you make this cut. The farther forward, the more the hindquarter will weigh. Next you can remove the quarters from the opposite half by cutting right down the center of the backbone with your saw. You now have two separate quarters on that side. Take each quarter and place it into a clean game bag. Now fold the clean hide that you carefully laid out back into its original position, roll the elk onto the side you just quartered and repeat the process for the opposite side.

13. Once you have removed and bagged all four quarters don't forget to remove the tastiest parts, the backstraps and the tenderloin. Backstraps are located along either side of the top of the spine. When cut they are long and triangular in shape. These should be carefully removed by making a longitudinal cut along each side of the spine followed by a second cut beneath each strap. Next look under the spine and with your knife remove the tenderloins, which lie in a similar location beneath the spine. These will be a bit shorter in length and round in shape. As this is my favorite part of the elk, I usually place these is a special bag all by themselves labeled, "if the airplane catches fire, save these first."

14. Depending upon your personal preference you can now remove any additional rib, neck or other meat that you like.

If it is a long hike back to camp and you will have to haul the meat out on your back, you may want to consider boning your meat out before you pack it out. It may take you a bit more time, but boning the meat out can save you from carrying as much as fifty pounds of unnecessary weight.

I prefer using heavy-duty cotton game bags as opposed to the lightweight cheesecloth type bags often used for deer. A bull elk hindquarter can easily go eighty pounds or more and experience had taught me that these lightweight bags just don't hold up as well as a set of sturdy cotton game bags.

Well you have had the fun part, experienced the messy part, and now the "less fun" part begins. That is hauling your elk back to camp. If you have boned the meat out, you can line your backpack with a regular large plastic trash bag, fill it with meat and begin your trek. If you have chosen to leave the bone in, securely lash a quarter to a good pack frame and start walking.

What about if you have to leave your elk or some part of your elk in the field? To protect the bagged quarters from birds or other critters I suggest hanging them from a limb in a cool spot in some trees. If there are no trees available look for some logs or limbs that you can rest the bagged quarter over. This will facilitate the cooling process while you are gone. Finally some hunters have been known to urinate around the site to discourage bears, wolves or coyotes from coming near the meat. For those of you who have yet to have this wonderful experience, this is one method of field dressing your elk.

Bringing It All Together

In this writer's experience elk hunting has proven to be one of the most challenging yet rewarding adventures that men and women can pursue. To be successful one must be willing to sacrifice much while achieving a level of commitment far beyond than which most sportsmen will ever attempt. Elk hunting is not merely the valiant pursuit of a worthy adversary; it is the realization of a passion God placed within each of us millions of years ago. A passion to step out into a wild and often perilous world, become one with those that inhabit this land, and return to the home fires with sustenance for our families, our souls enriched as a product of the adventure.

My prayer is that having made this book available to you; I will have passed along some amount of knowledge and experience, leaving you perhaps with something more than you started with. It has been my sincere pleasure writing this especially for you.

God Bless & Safe Hunting,
Jay

The realization of a passion is to step out into a wild and perilous world.

About the Author

Elk Hunting 201, Big Bulls... Essentials for a Successful Hunt is Jay Houston's second book in a three-book series on diverse aspects of Elk Hunting. His first book on this subject, *Elk Hunting 101, A Pocketbook Guide to Elk Hunting* released by Jackson Creek Publishers in the Spring of 2004 quickly became the fastest selling new book on elk hunting in America. Endorsed by the Rocky Mountain Elk Foundation *Elk Hunting 101* has helped thousands of elk hunters and would be elk hunters become more knowledgeable about this great adventure we call elk hunting.

A life-long big game hunter, elk hunting consultant, hunting guide, magazine editor and writer Jay has taken his passion for hunting and the outdoors and combined these with his fervent desire to pass on the knowledge and skill that he and others have acquired to those who will follow.

If you have enjoyed reading either of Jay's books on elk hunting, you will want to reserve your own copy of **Elk Hunting 301, Essays on the Adventure of Elk Hunting©**, due on bookshelves Summer 2006. *Elk Hunting 301* will include vivid personal accounts of tales from elk country written by authors who are consistently successful in this adventure. Follow their journeys as they stalk one of the most elusive big game animals on the planet. Learn from their mistakes as well as from their successes. Reserve your copy of *Elk Hunting 301, Essays on the Adventure of Elk Hunting* today. Email us at: elkmaster@ElkCamp.com.

About Our Cover Photographer

Jim Christensen

Though Jim's first true passion is wildlife photography, his portfolio abounds with landscapes, and abstract images. Jim's recent wildlife work was featured in a book published by AVA Switzerland, as well as a publication by Cornell University. His wildlife images have also appeared in Nikon advertisements, as well as professional brochures for non-profits and sportsmen's gear. Jim and his wife Reggie live in Duluth, Minnesota on the Western Tip of Lake Superior.

If you would like to learn more about Jim's work, he asks that you contact him at the address or email address below:

Digital Image Photography
222 Garden Street
Duluth, Minnesota 55812
Home: 218-728-6115
Cellular: 218-343-6510
E-Mail: N0exp@charter.net

Additional Photo Credits

Wayne Carlton: p.109
Kevin Fair: pp. 37
Danny Farris: pp.24, 26, 27, 29, 69, 89, 90, 96, 112, 116
Jay Houston: pp.9, 10, 12, 22, 46, 47, 58, 71, 73, 85, 117, 121, 127
Roger Medley: p.50, 138
Marc Smith: p.4,
Jerry Taylor: www.wildintherockies.com
    pp.11, 31, 32, 34, 36, 40, 57, 98, 137
Lindsay Williams: p.60

Bibliographic Resources

Bugling For Elk, Dwight Schuh, Stoneydale Press Publishing Company, Stevensville, MT, 1983

Big Game Hunter's Guide to Colorado, John Axelson, Wilderness Adventures Press, Inc., Belgrade, MT, 2002

Elk and Elk Hunting, Hart Wixom, Stackpole Books, Harrisburg, PA, 1986

Elk Hunting in the Northern Rockies, Ed Wolff, Stoneydale Press Publishing Company, Stevensville, MT, 1994

Elk Talk, Don Laubach & Mark Henckel, Falcon Publishing, Inc, Helena, MT, 1987

High Pressure Elk Hunting, Mike Lapinski, Stoneydale Press Publishing Company, Stevensville, MT, 1996

Hunt Elk, Jim Zumbo, New Win Publishing, Clinton, NJ, 1985

The Elk Hunter, Don Laubach & Mark Henckel, Falcon Publishing, Inc, Helena, MT, 1989

Literature Cited

[1] VerCauteren, Kurt C., and Pipas, Michael C. 2003. A review of color vision in white-tailed deer. Wildlife Society Bulletin 2003, 31 (3): 684-691.

Outstanding Resources for Gear and Services

The following are resources that we use personally. We highly recommend these companies for some of the best elk hunting gear and services you will find anywhere. Please consider these folks when you are in the market for your next hunt or piece of gear.

Alpen Optics
10329 Dorset St.
Rancho Cucamonga, CA 91730
Phone (909) 987-8370
Website: www.alpenoutdoor.com

Fossil Ridge Guide Service
Jim Michaud, Owner/Operator
9217 CR 76
Parlin, CO 81239
Phone (970) 641-5114
Website: www.fossilridgeguideservice.com

Magellan GPS
960 Overland Court, San Dimas, CA 91773
Phone: (800) 669-4477
Website: www.magellangps.com

Precision Shooting Equipment (PSE)
2727 N. Fairview Ave.
Tucson, Arizona 85705
Phone: (520) 884-9065
Website: www.pse-archery.com

Reliable Tent and Tipi Company
120 North 18th Street, Billings, MT 59101
Phone: (406) 252-4689
Website: www.reliabletent.com

Rusty Phelps Western Art
Phone: 719-495-9807
Website: www.rustyphelpswesternart.com

Wayne Carlton's CamoWest
104 South First Street
Montrose, CO 81401
Phone: (970) 240-2736
Website: www.camowest.com

Elk Hunting Notes